Town of Jacksonville
Oregon Territory

JACKSONVILLE, OREGON,
The Making of a National
Historic Landmark

UNITED STATES DEPARTMENT OF THE INTERIOR
WASHINGTON, D. C.

Jacksonville Historic District

Oregon

is hereby designated a

REGISTERED NATIONAL HISTORIC LANDMARK

*Under the Provisions of the
Historic Sites Act of August 21, 1935.
This Site Possesses Exceptional Value in
Commemorating and Illustrating the
History of the United States of America.*

Secretary of the Interior

Director, National Park Service

Jacksonville has had a Registered National Landmark District since 1966. See map showing boundaries of the historic area. The certificate reproduced here may be seen in the display case inside the entrance of the U.S. National Bank of Oregon's Jacksonville branch in the U.S. Hotel Building.

Jacksonville, Oregon,

THE MAKING OF A NATIONAL HISTORIC LANDMARK

BY

BERT AND MARGIE WEBBER

Ye Galleon Press
Fairfield, Washington

Library of Congress Cataloging in Publication Data

Webber, Bert,
    Jacksonville, Oregon, the making of a national historic landmark.

    Bibliography: p.
    Includes index.
    1. Jacksonville (Or.)—History. I. Webber, Margie. II. Title.
F884.J32W42   1982   979.5'25   82-13562
ISBN 0-87770-283-7
ISBN 0-87770-282-9 (pbk.)

Copyright (c) Bert Webber 1982
Printed in U.S.A.

Ye Galleon Press
Fairfield, Washington
99012

CONTENTS

Monument at corner S. Oregon and Applegate Streets
commemorates discovery of gold in 1851.

INTRODUCTION AND ACKNOWLEDGMENTS

Our first visit to Jacksonville was by accident, it was about 3 in the morning, and we were lost! The town was "different." We soon realized where we were because we'd read about it. The rented house we were looking for was about two miles back on a side road. We'd missed the turn.

Jacksonville intrigued us from the very start. Although it has not been our fortune to live there, the town is only minutes away from our home so visits are not unduly restricted. It's our favorite place to escort visitors.

What we did not learn about the town and its people from casual visits, we have surely learned during the research for the present book.

This book is intended as a popular volume for general reading but of reference value nevertheless. It is true here as with our other books, the background gleaned is immense when weighed against what finally emerges.

We talked informally with dozens of folks, and had formal interview appointments with others. We were in and out of the Reference Library at the Jacksonville Museum and the Reference Department of the Jackson County Library System in Medford on a continuing basis. At the Museum, Richard Engeman, librarian, assisted by Ida Clearwater, knew where data was kept on every subject we asked about and produced it with friendly professionalism whether we were there in person or at the end of a telephone line.

In the Medford Library Reference Department, Karen Chase (head), Connie Battaile and Shila Hungerford provided considerable help often by phone. In Jacksonville, public librarian Helen Roberts showed us artifacts which came with the building well over 100 years ago! We offer our heartfelt thanks to all of these librarians.

We quickly found the "center of contemporary information" in Jacksonville to be the City Hall, where Doris Crofoot and Peggy Breedlove fielded our questions with interest and precision, sometimes pointing out of a window and down the street toward what we were after. Now that's help!—for which we thank you.

Don Wendt receives a thank you and a handshake for his assistance with recollections of life in the town where he grew up and still calls home. As publisher of the *Jacksonville Nugget* (and a former city councilman) Don willingly provided much background and covered some matters about which we did not know to ask. He also set the "Old English" type used on the title page and front cover of this book on his newspaper's photo-typesetter.

Jacksonville's "Hungry '30's" backyard mining history is most colorful and was put together as we have it, after much help from fellows who were there: Wes Hartman and Bill Dobbyn. With Wes, we walked and drove the town and surrounding area stopping to view, then draw in locations of old mine shafts and tunnels under streets as he recalled them. Wes had been City Mining Inspector and Mayor. With Bill we went to Jackson Creek to look at the site where his gold dredge pulled out over $1,000 in some weeks. A very special acknowledgement and thanks to Mrs. A.C. Van Galder, who talked with us then showed us "dips" in her lawn—sites of former mine shafts.

Of assistance on the mining chapter was Novus Webb, who studied the mining history then put together the illustrated "Backyard Mining in Jacksonville" map published by the Southern Oregon Historical Society. Thank you all.

The treks we made through the brush and tall grass seeking evidence of the Rogue River Valley Railroad, and the people we talked with about that operation were most exciting. We found little had been written and that, sometimes faulty. But recollections were sharp from M. Dale Newton, railway historian and map maker who backed his comments with maps, photographs, and artifacts some of which are heretofore unpublished. And Newton was the one who pointed out the locations of many old rails used as street sign posts in Medford.

Wes Hartman rode that train many times—testified and helped us conclude that the right-of-way was no where near the steep grade others wrote about. Alvin Bowman, once Mayor and later land developer, validated our search for the place where the rails crossed Daisy Creek then proceeded east near Beverly Way. Stan Hobbs of the State Highway Engineer's Office, Medford, produced an old map which, early in our study, turned our heads in the direction that there was no steep grade between Medford and Jacksonville afterall. Fellows, thanks to you we have set the record and story straight.

There are so many persons who helped in various ways as April Sevcik of Pacific Northwest Bell Telephone, who sought data from a rare 1899 telephone book for us which added the little extra touch of flavor.

There is Rev. E. Melvin Kessinger and the Session of the First Presbyterian Church which permitted the two of us to scramble up narrow ladders into the belfry to photograph that great bell which has been announcing services almost continuously, weekly, for over 100 years.

And to Fr. Kruger and his willing helpers, Maria Carnagie and Dorothy King, who allowed us access into Parish archives and into the usually locked St. Joseph's Church, we appreciate the special time you took for which we thank you.

When one wants to locate a marker in a cemetery in a small town, it's important to meet the sexton, Wayne Maxon, without whom we'd have searched for days trying to locate monuments pertinent to our story.

Our search for facts and opinions throughout the Bear Creek Valley included: Eric Allen, Pat Blair, folks at the Britt Festival office, Ed Coffman, Robertson "Robbie" Collins, E.O. "Curley" Graham, George "Bud" Gregroy (Postmaster), Diane Fuhrmeister, Que Jameson, Mrs. George McCune, Russ McIntyre, Mike Moore, and Larry Smith, whose 6th grade class had done a picture history of the schools.

Historic postmarks add so much to the spirit of historical studies, so we asked Leonard Lukens to loan some of his choice "Jacksonville" cancellations which he graciously did.

There must be a friendly nod in the direction of Glen Cameron Adams, publisher, for his vision in recognizing this book as a contribution to the literature of the Pacific Northwest.

Thanks again to all of you.

Bert and Margie Webber
Central Point, Oregon
June 1982

ps: The authors are sensible that there may be some typographical and other errors in the following work; but as they will be found *few* and *inconsiderable*, it is not worthwhile to notice them.

B & M W (borrowed from Estwick Evans, 1819)

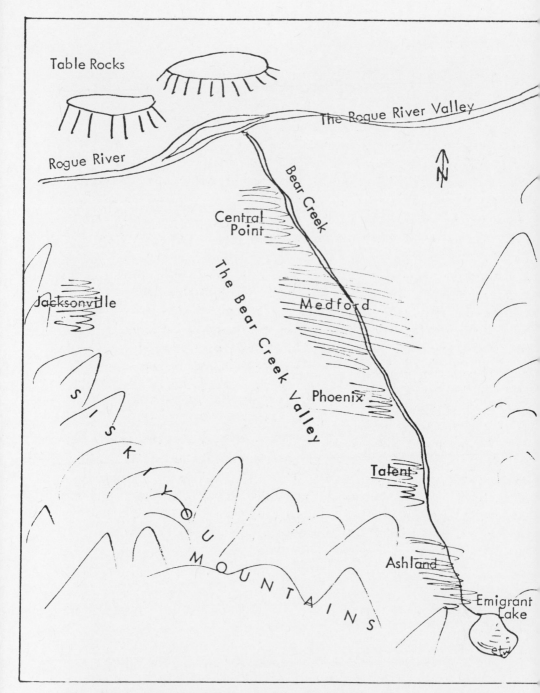

Table Rocks

The Rogue River Valley

Rogue River

N

Bear Creek

Central
Point

The Bear Creek Valley

Jacksonville

Medford

Phoenix

Talent

S I S K I Y O U   M O U N T A I N S

Ashland

Emigrant
Lake

Though it is common to refer to the area as the "Rogue Valley," to be more precise Jacksonville is in the "Bear Creek Valley."

CHAPTER 1

IN THE BEGINNING

OREGON'S HISTORIC LANDMARK DISTRICT IN JACKSONVILLE boasts a main street whose store buildings are over 100 years old and face on a street which may be lined with gold.

The city, about five miles west of Medford and in the foothills of the Siskiyou Mountains, got its start when gold was discovered in the area in 1851. Jacksonville is the oldest town in Southern Oregon and is a fascinating place to visit.

By the early 1850's, gold was the biggest news throughout the mountainous west. The strike had been immense near Sacramento and miners, who seldom stayed in one place very long, wandered north prospecting streams as they traveled. James Cluggage and John R. Pool found gold in Daisy Creek in Oregon, in the foothills of the Siskiyous. As the word got out, miners flocked to the area and a shanty town, Table Rock City, later Jacksonville, came into being.

The site of Jacksonville was in an almost unpopulated area. Oregon's first community was Astoria, at the mouth of the Columbia River, then settlements on the south side of the Columbia River sprang up near the confluence with the Willamette: Portland, Milwaukie, and Oregon City. The Willamette Valley was known for its fertile soil thus many immigrants, who sought new homes and wanted to farm, headed there in the great overland crossings. The boisterous shanty town of Jacksonville was almost 300 miles away on the raw frontier of Oregon.

A.G. Walling, writing in his *History of Southern Oregon* (published in 1884) recorded, "Nowhere else in America, possibly not in the world have the forces of nature so conspired to beautify and render a region thoroughly delightful as [here]."

Both Daisy Creek and Jackson Creek flow through the town. A few miles east is Bear Creek, the major drainage of the area, which empties into the Rogue River about eight miles to the north. Though it is common to refer to the area as the "Rogue Valley," to be more precise this is the Bear Creek Valley.

11

Earliest known picture of Jacksonville, probably late 1853, as the Methodist church is without steeple (white building in center). Shanty buldings in foreground house Chinese miners.

In early days, access to Jacksonville was rough for there are mountains on all sides. Some rise to 4,000 and 5,000 feet. Weather is mild with storm clouds spilling rain on the western slopes, then float over the valley to rain again on the next range.

Despite the fact that Jackson County was soon astride the stage coach route between Sacramento and the Willamette Valley, as well as being on the route of the South Road (Applegate Trail) from the mid-west, the area was considered far too remote a region for early development. Of course a major influx followed the electrifying news of "Gold"! Some early farmers had settled here and found ready markets for their produce among the miners of Jacksonville. The first log cabin was built in 1852. A large tent served as a general store, where the most common goods to trade for gold dust were whiskey, tools and heavy clothing.

The mines were described as "rich." Gambling, rough talk and booze

Jacksonville in mid-1850's. Note steeple on church, the church faced west on 4th Street. White "pyramid" near church was the "tent" built of split lumber by Rev. Joseph S. Smith, first Methodist minister and predates church. "Tent" was used as community hall for "court," as well as sermons. Long white building is Robinson House, a hotel with extension (compare with earlier town photograph). White building on far right in Jackson County's first Court House (note flag pole). The town also had the "Table Rock Bakery" (see sign at right). Chinatown in foreground.

were common while the sight of a woman—there were only five in the village—was a curiosity. Merchants from afar got the scent of potential business among the miners so these traders headed for the village. It was not long before several hundred people referred to Jacksonville as "home" during the week, but this swelled by several hundreds more on weekends as miners streamed into town from the hills. They headed for saloons, cardrooms, and the horse races. Business was brisk in the tent stores.

One enterprising fellow, John Ross, had roamed the frontier for years until he learned of the gold strike at Jacksonville. He quickly bought a herd of cattle in the Willamette Valley, moved them to a spot near Jacksonville, then he sold them to the miners for food.

In general, there appears to have been three types of people in early Jacksonville. 1) miners, 2) store keepers, 3) farmers. More often than not, farmers dealt directly with miners selling not only garden produce but beef, butter, eggs and pork. A blacksmith shop became a necessity and several smithies set up shops. The first plow manufactured in the Rogue Valley came from one of these forges.

Jacksonville, about 1860, southeast section. I.O.O.F. hall marked "A."

While miners roared in and out of town, others came to settle, do business and start families. Among them was 33-year-old Peter Britt to be followed shortly by Cornelius C. Beekman, about 25.

More than a few "well-disposed persons" had turned prospector, and when they rested on weekends, their homes became stopping places for itinerant preachers. Among these better-educated was Benjamin Franklin Dowell, schooled at the University of Virginia. He had become a lawyer but in Jacksonville he ran a pack train.

There was no organized law enforcement thus people were forced to cooperate for their mutual protection, particularly because the Indians were not yet settled. (*See*: Appendix A)

The Honorable Matthew P. Deady, United States District Judge for Oregon Territory by Presidential Appointment, held his first court in Jacksonville on September 5, 1853. One of the officers of his court was Lafayette F. Grover, who was a Lieutenant in the 1853 Rogue Indian War and went on to become the first U.S. Representative from the new State of Oregon, a Governor of Oregon, then U.S. Senator from Oregon.

Early in 1853, settlers included some who wished to start a Methodist Church. Among the very active in this movement was Rev. Joseph S. Smith (later a Representative to Congress), who had been assigned to the new

14

Early plat of Jacksonville. A: Planned site of Methodist Church which was built at A-1, later moved to B. C: Office of *Table Rock Sentinel* and presently the office of the *Jacksonville Nugget*. D: Catholic Church. E: Brunner Bros. store (today's library). F: Original City Hall. G: Cemetery. H: County Court House and jail (today's museum). I: Dairy Creek, also spelled "Dairey" on this map, later Daisy Creek. Historians believe it has always been Daisy Creek regardless of map designations. J: "A" Street has become Main Street. K: "B" Street was always known as California Street. L: "2nd" Street has always been known as Oregon Street (also Old Stage Road). M: Beekman Bank. N: Peter Britt Donation Land Claim (today's Peter Britt Gardens, a County Park). The plat was filed 1 September 1852 with the Jackson County Commissioners. (*See: Commissioners Journal* Vol. 1 Pg. 95)

village of Jacksonville, his wife, and two ladies, Miss Overbeck and Miss Emma Royal. These two women took to the mining camps and saloons to solicit money for a church. In town money was also collected from the "sporting fraternity" who in their own words were "hedging against bad fortune in the world to come."

In 1854 the Methodists built their church facing west on 4th Street. It was the first church in town. Later they turned it to face on 5th Street.

In the business world of the village, express service was opened to San

15

Early picture post card illustrating "Hydraulic Mining in Jackson
County, Oregon." Date unknown but postmarked at Tablerock,
Oregon, 1906.

Francisco via Yreka. Cornelius Beekman (called "Beek" by his friends)
rode horseback with gold dust from the miners and later carried letters.
Interestingly, Beekman traveled alone, was never held up, and crossed the
Siskiyous at night! He was later appointed Wells Fargo agent for
Jacksonville and eventually, in 1857, founded the first bank in Southern
Oregon. Beekman became one of Jacksonville's most distinguished and
philanthropic citizens.

The first child was born in Jacksonville on August 5, 1853 to Doctor
and Mrs. McCully. It was noted by one historian that the boy, who was
named James Cluggage McCully for the town's founder, became the
special pride of many miners and traders—all claiming to be
godfathers—"and made it their especial business to spoil the graceless little
scamp and teach him lessons that required years of Sunday School
attendance to eradicate."

It should be pointed out that the major type of mining in Jacksonville
at this time was "placer" mining. Such mining can be done when gold-
bearing sand and gravel settle out from rapidly moving streams at places

16

where the streams slow down. Panning for gold requires a wide, flat pan into which a few handfuls of dirt (which the prospector hopes contains gold), and a large amount of water have been placed. By swirling the contents the miner washes the dirt and sand over the edge of the pan leaving any heavy matter, including gold, if any, in the pan. After several washings of the same handful of dirt, only gold and other heavy metals are left. "Nuggets," as different from "dust," can be picked out of the pan with fingers. If there is only dust present, continuous washing is needed to force all of the dirt over the edge of the pan. When only dust remains, the miner carefully removes the particles, sometimes with tweezers, or a knife blade, from the pan.

Traditionally, gold prospectors work a stream looking for "color" only for a short time in any one spot. They move about dipping their pan here and there. If a stream produces, they stay until they can't find any more. In the California strike, placer mining lasted just a short while—until surface gold in the streams was panned out. In Jacksonville, the same procedure was followed with many miners moving on after a relatively short stay. As miners left, others came in. The turnover does not seem to be recorded but it was heavy. White miners, when compared with Chinese miners, did an incomplete job. Whites seemed to discourage easily then moved on but the Chinese, as we shall see, reworked several times over the very spots which whites had abandoned.

Summer of 1853 was most eventful: additional gold discoveries brought more and more people. It was a season of great prosperity. Goods were mule train packed over 100 miles from the seaport at Crescent City, California. An uneasy treaty was made with the Indians to patch up past quarrels, thus many felt that Indian trouble was lessened. (*Authors' note:* The present book will mention the Rogue Indians Wars only in passing. *See:* Appendix A for an opinion at the time.)

Much gold poured into Jacksonville and summer nights were never quiet! Walling wrote, "There never was a mining camp where personal liberty was less restrained, better enjoyed or less abused than in Jacksonville in '53." We wonder if Mr. Walling was actually describing Jacksonville, *Oregon?*

With "civilization" growing in this shanty town in the foothills of the Siskiyous, crime was also growing. Rape, theft, murder filled the docket of the court. Indian trouble was brewing following the arrest of three

17

Indians, each on separate murder charges. Each was tried and found guilty. All three were publicly hanged. Jacksonville was surely no quiet, country village at this time.

Life was hard work day after day in this far-flung corner of America and the settlers, as well as the miners, longed for their friends and loved ones who had remained at home thousands of miles away. Their contact with the "doings" of the world they had left behind was eagerly kept via mailorder newspapers.

Welborn Beeson confided to his diary on Dec. 15, 1853, that he had struck a deal with a neighbor, John Meall, for each to fetch the others' papers and letters from Jacksonville when either was in that village. Beeson lived on his father's farm near what is now the City of Talent, about ten miles southeast. At one point Beeson wrote he hated to spend the dollar for a subscription to a distant paper as money was very dear, but he felt he couldn't get along without it.

After the passage of the Donation Land Act which promised free, fertile farm land, the population increased with those who wanted to build homes and stay.

As gold mining declined, skeptics announced the end of the town was near. True, the restless left, but that was nothing new. Some puttered around the creeks or took jobs with businesses which were starting to grow.

The businessmen of the town began to look to the farmers for support.

The adjustment from a local "gold dust standard" to an economy supported by less immediately-available cash but from steadily-employed farmers was uneasy. The mines had been the initial incentive for many of the agricultural ventures and when the farmers did their buying, it was with gold dust or coin realized from direct sales to the miners. Fewer miners, less ready cash flow. It took a farmer many weeks, sometimes months from seed to harvested crop. For orchards, the investment was great with no proceeds for several years.

But farmers were prospering more than most realized. After the first few hard winters, the valley was largely self-sufficient. By the time the mines ran out—about ten years—farmers were looking for out-of-area markets. Centers-of-interest were appearing in the county. Ashland Mills and Phoenix had flour mills. Jacksonville became the banking and shipping center, was the county seat and had a newspaper, the *Table Rock Sentinel*. There were nearly a dozen merchants with substantial

18

establishments in town, many saloons, and even a bowling alley! An hotel, the Robinson House—on the site of the present United States Hotel—catered to all who were stuck in town overnight. In additon, there was a boarding house of a more elite nature (in which some of the courtesans abided). There were many small businesses including two bakers, a stable and a furniture maker.

In contrast to the mule packers and miners, people in town took on a refinement in manners of dress. "Boiled shirts" became the fashion for young gents if they were to make any headway with the increasing crop of young ladies.

Emma Royal, who had been one of the money collectors for funds to build the Methodist Church, opened the first school in the winter of 1853 and funded it in part by returning to the miners for more gold dust contributions.

Winters were severe. With narrow trails and no roads, snow obscured the landscape and supplies ran low. Salt and flour were always short in winter so neighbors shared for as long as supplies lasted.

PRICES IN JACKSONVILLE MAY 27, 1854

Men's Shoes $2.50	Shirts $1	Pants $2	Muslin 25ᶜ-yd	Milk Pail $1
Sharpening stone $1	Sack of salt $1	Sugar 34ᶜ-lb.	Calico 24ᶜ-yd	Nails 35ᶜ-lb.

On September 9, 1854, Welborn Beeson hauled farm produce to Jacksonville to sell. He got 12½ᶜ lb. for 600 lbs. flour, 6ᶜ lb. for 300 lbs. potatoes.

Suitable clay had been found near Jacksonville and a brick kiln was set up, resulting in the first brick building being constructed in 1854. (That building stood twenty years then burned and the brick walls collapsed.)

The Methodist Church and Miss Emma Royal's school prospered, although that first school term lasted only one month. As Walling wrote concerning the first Roman Catholic overtures in the area, "It would have been strange, indeed, if so promising a field had been overlooked by the Roman Catholic arch-bishop of Oregon."

Rev. Fr. James Croke, a missionary of Oregon's arch-diocese, arrived in Jacksonville in September 1853 for a look-see. While in the village he celebrated mass in a private residence. Here, historian Walling claims Fr. Croke found "a strong steadfast and faithful Catholic society."

The Brunner Brothers built the second brick building in town which still stands, is now public library.

But Father Croke's report to his headquarters described the Jacksonville "parish" in slightly stronger words:

The Catholics here are so few and in general so lukewarm that it requires some time for a priest to hunt them out.
— Catholic History of Oregon

In all of the Rogue Valley, Fr. Croke could count only "100 Catholic adults and 5 minors."

The second brick building in Jacksonville came into existence also in 1854 when the Brunner Brothers erected it for their store. This building still stands and houses the Jacksonville Branch of the Jackson County Library System. An original writing desk remains in the building and is used daily by librarian and patrons.

Another brick building, the Masonic Lodge, was built in 1855.

A long feared and bloody Indian war became a reality, when unsettled Indians and troublesome whites met in deadly skirmishes throughout the valley and into the foothills of the Siskiyous. There was no militia to call so the men left wives and firesides to shoulder what arms they could muster to fight Indians. On Octorber 8, a company, organized at Jacksonville, attacked an Indian camp on Butte Creek and killed most of the band, which consisted mostly of old men, women and children. The Indians went on the warpath and killed at least 23 whites immediately

20

Methodist Church in 1982. Building sold to City of Jacksonville for $300 in 1937, administered by Southern Oregon Historical Society. Presently rented to another denomination.

thereafter. There never was an attack in Jacksonville itself, but the anxiety, especially among the wives and young girls who imagined themselves being carried off by what they believed would be uncouth, sweat-stained savages, was continual. When there were threats of Indian attacks, Jacksonville folklore tells that the women often barricaded themselves in Brunner's brick store. The wives wanted their men to stay home and they said so.

Some of these women met in an indignation meeting in the Methodist Church about their men abandoning them and roaring around fields looking for Indians. The women passed a resolution denouncing their men's actions. Showing little respect for their ladies' wrath, some fellows late one night hoisted a petticoat to the town's flag pole. (It was later hauled down amidst a flurry of the women.)

Interior, Jacksonville Branch, Jackson County Public Library System in original Brunner Bros. building on S. Oregon Street.

(Left) Brunner Bros. Building in 1982, houses Public Library. On right is Orth Building, vacant in 1982.

CALIFORNIA & OREGON STAGE COMPANY.
CARRIES WELLS FARGO & CO! EXPRESS AND THE U.S. MAIL.
VIEW OF MOUNT SHASTA 14,442 FT ABOVE THE SEA- ON C.& O. STAGE ROUTE.

Artists loved to picture spirited horses racing ahead of a loaded stage coach. In reality, coach could seat only 9 passengers, usually none on top other than driver and "shotgun" in bench seat.

Welborn Beeson's Diary:

APRIL 27, 1855

We Went to Jacksonville. took potatoes butter and eggs, We heard a speech at the Robison (sic) [Dr. Robertson] house by Gen. Joseph Lane, who is a candidate for Representative to Congress. he is a red man with whiskey roses all on his nose. he is a Demicrat. We also heard a speech from Gen Gainer, a Whig Candidate fir the same he is a white haired old man living on the Columbia [River]. It rained on us as we came home.

Within four years Jacksonville had four lawyers, several doctors and merchants of a general variety. Leaders were beginning to emerge who would become the mainstay of the community both in business and politics.

Early religious leaders centered on Jacksonville due to its larger population, but soon worked throughout the county. The Methodists, Catholics, Presbyterians and Baptists came, all wanting to build permanent establishments. The Baptists, who appeared to lack sufficient numbers as well as funding from the east, never gained a foothold and there isn't a Baptist Church in Jacksonville in 1982. We will discuss the others in due time.

Jacksonville, despite its growth and genesis of of stability was still a frontier town. Railroads were becoming numerous in the east, but to get in or out of "J'ville," one could walk, ride a horse — possibly with a wagon — or take a stage coach. Riding the stage with its attendant uncomfortable mountain passes, strained the stoutest horses and the stress limits of passengers. Summers were unbearable with dust, and winters were freezing to all who sat and bounced or became "seasick" with the sway. None but the hardiest or those whose business absolutely required it, took the stage. □

THE TABLE ROCK SENTINEL.

BY TVAULT & BLAKELY.]

INDEPENDENT ON ALL SUBJECTS; DEVOTED TO THE BEST INTERESTS OF SOUTHERN OREGON.

[TERMS—$5 00 PER ANNUM.

Volume 4.

JACKSONVILLE, OREGON, SATURDAY, MAY 24, 1850.

Number 27.

THE TABLE ROCK SENTINEL

IS PUBLISHED EVERY SATURDAY, BY

TVAULT & BLAKELY.

Terms—In Advance:

One copy, for one year, $5 00.
"   "   six months, $3 00.
"   "   three months, $2 00.

ADVERTISEMENTS

Will be inserted at the following rates: One square of twelve lines or less, three insertions, $3 00; each subsequent insertion, $1 00. A liberal deduction made to yearly advertisers.

Business Cards, of ten lines or less, for one year, $20; to persons who advertise to the extent of three squares or more, a reduction of 50 per cent, will be made.

☞ The number of insertions must be distinctly marked on the margin, otherwise they will be continued till forbidden, and charged accordingly.

Chinese News.

Our exchanges by the Live Yankee did not come to hand till yesterday morning. We cannot find any news of importance in them, except the following from the Hong-kong *Register* of the 11th March.

THE AMERICAN MINISTER'S BUSINESS.—We have been informed that some amusing epistolary diplomatic bye-play has lately taken place between H. E. Dr. Parker, the American Commissioner, and Hip, the Viceroy of Canton. We have not seen the correspondence, but it has been made public enough to warrant our alluding to it, as it is as follows:

On the Commissioner's arrival by the December mail, H. E. addressed a communication to Hip, informing him of his having entered upon the duties of his office as Commissioner from the United States—expressing his pleasure at finding the country free from the civil dissensions which had existed on his departure—assuring Hip of the high consideration in which the Court of China would regard him—"thousand vows"

News Items Crowded Out Last Week.

DISTRESSING ACCIDENT.—A very distressing accident occurred yesterday afternoon, at half-past five o'clock, at Pacific Garden, which cast a shadow over the Turner's Festival. A man named Charles Degers and a Hollander, name unknown, were engaged in firing a salute with a brass four-pounder on the grass plat in front of the garden. They were ramming home the charge for the third discharge when the charge exploded, horribly mutilating both the parties. Degers had his right hand blown entirely off, lost his left arm below the elbow joint, besides the muscle of his left shoulder, the fleshy portion of his throat, and a wound in the left breast. The Hollander had both of his hands blown off, but was not injured otherwise bodily. The wounded men presented a most pitiful spectacle. The Chief Engineer, Mr. Nutiman, and his Assistants, Mr. Devoe, Mr. Walsh, the Foreman of Engine Company No. 8, together with the reporters of the press and other active gentlemen present, rendered prompt and sympathetic attention to the wounded men. Degers was carried to the German Benevolent Infirmary, on Mission street, near Third, and received the best medical attention by Dr. Sawyer, Physician to the Fire Department, assisted by Drs. C. J. Bryant and J. J. Cushing. At a late hour last evening he was still alive, although his recovery under such mutilation is almost impossible. The Hollander was taken to a private house, where he is under the treatment of Drs. Gray and Harris. It is more than probable he will recover.—*S. F. Herald, 6th.*

ROBBERY.—A miner who had taken passage yesterday on the steamer Sierra Nevada, was robbed of $7,000. He

"Some Shaking."

Tom is a queer genius, and lots of some tall ones occasionally. He visited us the other day in our sanctum, with a

"How do you do, old fellow?"

"Hallo, Tom," said we, "where have you been so long?"

"Why, sir, I have been down on Seven River, in Anne Arundel county, taking shanghai noises on the chills and fevers."

"Ah, indeed; are they very bad down there?"

"Rather bad," said Tom, drily. "There is one place where they have been attempting to build a brick house for eight weeks—well, the other day, as the hands were putting up the bricks preparatory to finishing it, they were taken with a chill and shook till the bricks were dust of the finest quality! Just at that juncture the chills came on with renewed force and, they commenced shaking up the dust with such gusto that the people of the neighborhood thought the sun was in an eclipse."

"Can't believe anything like that, Tom."

"It's a fact," said Tom, and resumed:

"There's a farmer down there, who, in apple-picking season, hauls his niggers out to the orchard and sets one up against each tree on the ground."

"Incredible!" said we, holding our sides with both hands.

"Fact," said Tom, "they keep a man alongside of each negro to catch the fruit as soon as they jostle it off, for fear he will shake the tree down."

Tom continued, "Mrs. S—— friend of mine, had a carpenter, who was engaged a few days ago in covering the roof of a house with shingles. Just as he was 'finishing,' the chill came on and he shook every shingle off the roof. Some of them was supposed to be flying about yet."

"Another gentleman, near the same place, was taken with a chill the other day at din-

GLAD I DON'T GET MARRIED.—We take the following from the *Evening Bulletin* of the 10th inst:

"Well, I'm an old maid! Not the only one, either, thank Heaven! To be sure, there's not a superabundance in San Francisco—reasons enough why there 'aint, too. I do really believe it's the greatest market for girls, young or old, in the known world. Now there isn't a city, town or village this side the Himalayas, but what has shipped more or less of this stock—always ready sale—plenty of buyers, with the cash in hand. Wasn't I mad, after having my stomach turned inside out, on that rolling, shaking *George Law*—almost breaking my neck up and down those fearful mountains, on a cross-grained, superannuated mule, and then drawing the breath of life three whole weeks in a little square place, half as large as an old Tim's dog kennel—I say, wasn't I mad when I got here, to find there wasn't a young man, widower or bachelor in the whole place worth having? Now, I'm as reasonable a woman as ever was born, since Mrs. Eve let the light of her eyes shine upon poor lonely Adam, but I'd no more think of marrying one of those miserable, pleasure seeking lovers of mammon, than worshipping that molten calf the Good Book tells about! No! I! I've got a few hundred left yet—if it did cost a heap to rig out, and land here! I am glad enough I wasn't in a hurry. The best thing I ever did in all my life, was taking a fancy to a single life, when an old maid, eh!—yes, indeed! Do you think I'd sell my freedom to a 'regular Californian! I've always had some domestic notions, whenever matrimony was thought of. What, marry a man who never lives in a house except when asleep!—forever out—though the fog is so thick he can't see his own nose, or

A HARD SHELL BURIEL SERMON.—The *Baltimore American* has received from a friend in Lexington, Ky., the following "Hard Shell Sermon," which he avers to be genuine. It about equals, in closeness of argument and strict adherence to the text, the "spontaneous efforts" of the clerical hero who played upon a "harp of a thousand strings"

"My brethring: The Scripture tell us, 'we are *buried* with Christ by baptism.' *Buried*,' my friends, not '*sprinkled*' by baptism.

"Suppose that one of you had lost your little darter, and you had laid her out, and proposed now for the grave; and your neighbors had come in and said: 'Friend, we will take thy child and bury it,' and afterward, when you went out to see the grave of your little one, you found they had half laid her down and *sprinkled* a little earth over her! What would you have thunk of them?

"Suppose, again, that in the fall of the year, you had dug your potatoes, your turnips, your parsnips and your other roots for winter's use, and had dug a trench to bury 'em in; and you had said to your servant: 'Sally, take the house gang and go and bury these potatoes, these turnips, these parsnips and other roots;' and afterward, when you walked forth to see that all were secure for the winter's use, you had found that they had just *sprinkled* a little dirt on them! What my friends would you have done? I rather suppose, my dear brethren, you would ha' tried the virtues of the cow-skin!

"But they are not a bit worse than those poor, ignorant, benighted Episcopalians and Presbyterians and Methodists, who sprinkle a leetle water on one another and call it 'baptized by baptism'

"I am afraid, my friends, I am very much afraid indeed, that they will catch something better than the cow-skin in the day of reckoning!"

PEN, PASTE AND SCISSORS.

(Principally Scissors.)

What do we often drop, but never stoop to pick up? A hint.

Men are called sons of guns because they all go off—some time or other.

The bumps raised on a man's head by a cudgel are called *frey-nological developments.*

☞ What marine excrescence is a man like who lives idly upon his friends? A sponge.

A correspondent asks whether the "bridge of the nose" is a suspension or tubular bridge?

If you wish to know whether anybody is superior to the prejudices of the world, ask him to draw a truck for you.

A lazy fellow down South spells Tennessee thus: 10d. Jackson is the fellow who spells Arkansas thus—Ext Jxrs.

A recent philosopher discovers a method to avoid being dunned. "How? how!" we hear everybody asking. Never run in debt.

Says the lovely Ellen to the bewitching Fanny, "why is a new baby like a cocktail? Fanny blushed as she answered, "because it was never seen *before.*"

"Mr. Smith, you said you boarded at the Columbian Hotel six months, did you foot your bill?" No, sir; but it amounted to the same thing—he landlord footed me."

An Irishman, writing to a friend from the West, remarked, that "Pork is so plenty here that every third man you meet is a hog."

A correspondent asks, whether the young lady who fell in love recovered, or did she sink into the unfathomable depths of matrimony?

CONFESSION OF AN UGLY MAN.—Women

CHAPTER 2

A FONT OF PRINTERS

A TOWN'S PROGRESS MIGHT BE MARKED AS SUBSTANTIAL WITH the arrival of a newspaper. Now, 1855, William Green T'Vault, with "Messers Taylor and [Alex] Blakeley," hauled a printing press from a defunct paper at Scottsburg in Douglas County's Umpqua Valley to Jacksonville. They started the *Table Rock Sentinel*. This was the first newspaper in Southern Oregon. (Earlier, and for a very short time, the village had been called Table Rock for a nearby promontory.) T'Vault, the obvious leader and a lawyer, in time bought out his partners. He was somewhat stern in his feelings about many things, especially Indians, having participated in the Rogue Indian War of 1853 "with no great glory," according to Turnbull.

On the top of the page of each issue of his paper, T'Vault displayed this statement: "INDEPENDENT ON ALL SUBJECTS; DEVOTED TO THE BEST INTERESTS OF SOUTHERN OREGON." He had a lively paper! He republished articles from papers in San Francisco, Hong Kong, the Puget Sound region, as well as new material picked up from travelers. He ran advertising including his own: "W.G. T'Vault, Attorney and Counsellor at Law."

"T'Vault," wrote Walling, "was a man of ability and force of character, compensating for lack of culture by force of will, uncompromising in his animosities, but fair to his friends."

He had been in charge of a small band of volunteers during the Indian War. While on an overland march through Douglas County, he chose a place for an overnight camp against the advice of one of his men. Earlier, the man had been involved in an Indian attack at this very place and told T'Vault not to camp there. T'Vault, being "Colonel" and assertively exhibiting his power as commander, decided to camp at the site anyway. During the night the little group was furiously attacked while they slept, nearly all being wounded or killed. T'Vault escaped through the brush unhurt but was obviously gun-shy of Indians ever afterward.

Jacksonville Nugget

SERVING THE RESIDENTS OF JACKSONVILLE, RUCH, AND APPLEGATE VALLEY

WEEK DECEMBER 11-17, 1981.

FREE WEEKLY PUBLICATION
MAILED TO ALL RESIDENTS IN
JACKSONVILLE AND APPLEGATE

VOL. 5. NO.

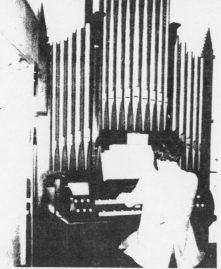

Alan Collins, a Medford organist, held a brief recital at the Jacksonville Museum during dedication services for the newly restored reed organ first in use in 1893.

Photo By Vella Munn

New Life Pumped Into Peloubet Organ

Dedication Held At Museum

by Vella Munn

A hand-pumped Peloubet Organ from the Lyon and Healy Company of Chicago has resided in the Jacksonville Museum. Now, as the result of fund raising efforts by two museum employees, the organ is no longer religated to a silent corner of the room.

On December 4 the organ was officially dedicated. The highlight of the afternoon was a short recital performed by Alan Collins, a prominent Medford organist who recently returned from study at the New England Conservatory in Boston. Before his recital Collins admitted that as a boy he slipped into the museum and played the then hand-pumped organ. The 'deed' was discovered since it's hard to deny something when no one else is in the room. Instead of being asked to leave, Collins

was invited to sit dow play.

Collins found it much to perform this time there is no longer the ne of 'bribing' someone, u a boy, to work the pump.

The organ was dona 1956 by Mr. and Mrs. C of Phoenix in the mem Mrs. Ruth Clafflin, Mr Claflin, and Mr. and L.O. Caster. Early in Catherine Wendt, recept at the museum and Jody then collections registrar ched a memorial fund f restoration of the two-m reed organ. Dottie B Administrative Assistan ted as coordinator of th ding for the restoration paign. The total resto cost was around one tho

CONTD. PAG

OFFICER SUSPENDED BEFORE RESIGNATION

Police Officer Eric Bennett Leaves City Post Plans Return To Texas

by Vella Munn

Eric Bennett's tenure as a Jacksonville policeman has been a stormy one. When the former El Paso cop was hired in August Vic Clime was acting chief. When Bennett learned that Mike Moore had been recommended as permanent chief over Clime and several other candidates Bennett called a news conference

during which he outlined his objections to Moore's appointment. 'For the same money as the city is paying for Mike it can get the best in the state,' Bennett said. 'I don't know what Mike has.' Bennett was upset because Clime and another candidate had

CONTD. PAGE 3

BULK RATE
POSTAGE PAID
PERMIT NO. 19.
JACKSONVILLE,
OR 97530

CAR - RTE.

Local Postal Patron
Jacksonville Local
Route 1-Jacksonville
Route 2-Jacksonville
Route 3-Jacksonville
Route 4-Jacksonville
Applegate Station

There was a farmer by name of John Beeson, who had a spread near the present City of Talent, some ten miles from Jacksonville. Beeson was very disturbed at the barbaric treatment the Indians were receiving at the hands of settlers and said so. Beeson was frequently on business in J'ville" with his son, Welborn, and while there spoke to all who would listen. After many corner speeches, along with Beeson-written articles about brutalilty to Indians which T'Vault discovered were being printed in San Francisco papers, T'Vault, along with several others, called an "indignation meeting" in Beeson's neighborhood. In short, John Beeson was threatened to where he feared for his life. Thus, late one night, he abandoned his wife, son, and farm to flee the country. (John Beeson's story appears in the Ye Galleon Press book *A Plea for the Indians*, with Introduction by Bert Webber, in which will be found very colorful details of Beeson's many years fighting for Indian rights.)

Over the next several years T'Vault's paper changed names, partners and owners several times. In 1859 it became *Oregon Sentinel* but closed shop in 1861. The paper had been intensely Democrat and at times so radical that citizens loyal to the Union refused to buy or read it. Accordingly, the paper's financial matters became untenable.

In the meantime in 1857, following a notion that if a community would support one paper two would be better, two men started the *Jacksonville Herald*. The *Herald* underwent more changes than did the *Sentinel* and lasted a very short time. When the *Sentinel* folded, its plant was used by Messers O'Meara and Pomeroy to start the *Southern Oregon Gazette*. One historian reported that the *Gazette's* editorial policy was so disloyal to the government that very shortly it was refused use of the United States Mail! Thus, the *Gazette* died quickly for the mail was the major manner of circulation.

The next paper for Jacksonville was the *Civilian*, also Democrat but of a much milder form. Readers had been burned by Democrat editors so the *Civilian* was unpopular—died. In 1863 T'Vault took possession of the *Civilian* and changed it to the *Intelligencer*, but that paper didn't pay so T'Vault quit the publishing business and gave all of his time to his law office.

The *Oregon Reporter* arose from the ashes of its predecessors in January 1865, but that too failed within a year. Under new ownership, the *Reporter* hit the streets in 1867 but changed the name to *Southern Oregon*

Press. This lasted several months, to be followed by the *Reveille* which also had a short stand. In 1869 the *Democratic News* came out under the leadership of P.D. Hull and Charles Nickell. The paper was just getting its feet on the ground when the plant burned in the fire of 1872. As quickly as new money was available, the *Democratic Times* was started by Nickell and survived to the turn of the century when it was consolidated with the *Southern Oregonian.* In 1906 a weekly, the *Post,* came along. This paper appeared at a time of less national controversy and lasted many years. There is mention of another paper, the *Miner,* in 1933, in Francis D. Haines Jr.'s book *JACKSONVILLE; Biography of a Gold Camp.*

For a short time the *Weekly Independent* was published, then there was the *Sentinel-American* in 1963.

At the present time (1982) the *Jacksonville Nugget,* a weekly, contains local news and local business ads. The major papers circulated in Jacksonville in 1982 are the Medford *Mail Tribune;* two Portland papers, the *Oregonian* and *Oregon Journal*;* and the San Francisco *Chronicle.* □

---

* *As this book is going to press authors learn the* Oregonian *and* Oregon Journal *will be combined into a single paper in September 1982,* Oregonian *surviving.*

California Street 1982. Building on right is original office of T'Vault's *Table Rock Sentinel.* Today is office of Jacksonville *Nugget* as well as import gift and souvenier shop.

Rev. Moses A. Williams, founding Presbyterian missionary-minister, later Supt. of Jackson County Schools.

CHAPTER 3

STEPS FORWARD

FOR AWHILE, JACKSONVILLE WAS THE LARGEST CITY IN OREGON (Walling p. 342). There was express service, stage lines and mail. There were local merchants and a banker—C.C. Beekman. In 1856, Beekman reported that the "diggins" yielded close to $1,500,000—the greatest haul for a single year during the approximately ten years the gold lasted. After 1856, as surface ore dwindled, it became necessary for heavy mining equipment to extract the gold. Experienced prospectors realized that easy-panning had passed, so they too passed from the scene.

The first Presbyterian missionary, Moses Williams, arrived in 1857

First Presbyterian Church constructed in 1881 and in use continuously. Presbyterian services started in 1857 sharing the Methodist's building. Bell in Presbyterian Church has been heralding worship services for over 100 years.

and preached his first sermon in a school house near what was later to become the city of Ashland. Reverend Williams was commonly called "Father," because "he looked patriarchal and spoke like a prophet." He formally organized the first Presbyterian Church in Southern Oregon at Jacksonville that year. As the Presbyterians had not yet erected a building, the Methodists shared theirs and later formed The Union Sunday School together. This cooperation continued until the Presbyterians opened their own building in 1881.

Williams, educated at Columbia and Princeton Theological Seminaries, was ordained for the Presbytery of Georgia in 1846. Although he settled in Ashland, he formed Presbyterian Churches in Jacksonville, Phoenix, Ashland, Medford and in Eagle Point. He probably married more couples than any minister in his thirty years' residence in Jackson County. One of the best educated men in the area, he thought highly of public schools. He was elected County Superintendent of Schools while active in church work. Williams divided the county into school districts which, for the most part, remain intact today. He strongly advocated Bible reading in the schools and there did not seem to be open discontent about this. During official visits to schools as Superintendent, he gathered children about him and told Bible stories. "Father" Williams died in 1887 and was buried in Jacksonville's cemetery.

With more and more and more people settling in and around town, and with a strong influx of merchants representing all types of goods, the muddy trails (loosely called "streets"), had to be improved. In the early '60's, the town council decided to grade the streets. A major thoroughfare, the "stage road," went through Jacksonville from Rock Point on the Rogue River via Willow Springs (west of Central Point), then through Phoenix to Ashland, and on over the Siskiyous.

As mentioned earlier, the nearest sea port was Crescent City, about 100 miles away. The lonesome, winding trail over mountains and through deep valleys was a hard pull. Making the trips were swarthy mule skinners who exacted a goodly fee in exchange for their hard and often frustrating work.

A thriving village, Sailor Diggings (later Waldo) where sailors, who had jumped ship at Crescent City, had discovered gold in 1852, became a major stopping place. By the summer of 1860 a greatly improved wagon road was completed between Waldo and the coast. Freight wagons, with as many as two heavily loaded trailers pulled by 16 to 18 horses, hauling as much as thirty tons of goods, plodded along the road. To avoid head on collisions on the narrower sections, bells were attached to the lead horses. It's been said that those living along the road could identify a team before it came into sight by their different bell tones. The better road and easier travel lowered prices on goods destined for Jacksonville. Along with this improvement, the Mexican mule packers slowly went out of the packing business and left the scene. During this period, a twice-weekly stage coach carried passengers between the coast and Jacksonville, as well as express and probably mail.

R. Dugan opened the Jacksonville Post Office on February 18, 1854 at a time when the Post Office Department was experienceing rapid expansion. For years, letters were sent to Post Offices the writers knew to be near where their emigrant family members and friends had settled. In the Bear Creek Valley, it was common for letters to turn up in any of several Post Offices where neighbors stopped regularly on every trip to town seeking mail for themselves as well as for friends. Before the publishing of the *Table Rock Sentinel*, the only newspapers in the area came as mail subscriptions, from many settlers' old home towns in the east.

The California Stage Company, which had been operating from Portland through the Willamette Valley and on to Sacramento, stopped in Jacksonville. In 1860 the firm was awarded a mail contract over this long route. Comfortable (?) four-horse stages became a daily sight in Jacksonville and shortened the arduous travel time. But the coaches were usually overcrowded. Many tired and dusty passengers looked forward to a rest—often overnight—in the hotels of "J'ville," poor as they were. □

CHAPTER 4

ST. JOSEPH'S PARISH

S NOTED EARLIER, THE CATHOLICS HAD EXPLORED Southern Oregon in 1853. Following this, they sent priests annually into the Jacksonville area. Archbishop Norbert Blanchet, of Oregon City, had once made the rough trip over the mountains in October 1858, and while in Jacksonville, he contracted for the construction of a church on a piece of donated land in the center of town. Work started in 1859 after founding Father Croke had collected "in cash $856" from miners and others as far as 65 miles away reporting, "this was very fortunate for otherwise I could scarcely collect only $30 in Jacksonville. They all promise and will give their names very readily to be paid at some future day, but names won't build a church."

The building under way, Fr. Croke wrote, "The church looks very high and when completed will be a neat building...it is 36x23."

Then he left town on priestly work in Yreka, California. On his return, he complained that after having been gone awhile, "I was surprised to find so little done to the church during my absence. The carpenters give excuses...."

The first services were apparently held in 1859, then in 1860 Archbishop Blanchet visited Southern Oregon a second and last time offering Mass from the little church. By 1861 a parish priest had been appointed, Rev. J.T. Fierens, with residence in Jacksonville. A house was found near the church and arrangements were made to use it as a rectory. Fr. Fierens stayed until late November 1863 when he left for Portland. There he built a cathedral and served out the rest of his life.

Fr. Fierens' replacement was the Rev. Francoise Xavior Blanchet, a nephew of the Archbishop. Under Fr. F.X. Blanchet's guidance, the parish grew and became consolidated.

In the meantime, as we have seen, the Methodists and Presbyterians were quite busy and had started the Union Sunday School. We also recall that Emma Royal held school classes. Fr. Blanchet was convinced that Catholic education was needed, so he asked for a contingent of nuns from Montreal with which to start a school. The school, to be called St. Mary's Academy, opened in 1865. We note that

St. Joseph's Roman Catholic Church. Second house of worship to be constructed in Jacksonville (1859).

Interior, St. Joseph's Catholic Church. Archbishop Francis Norbert Blanchet said Mass here in 1860.

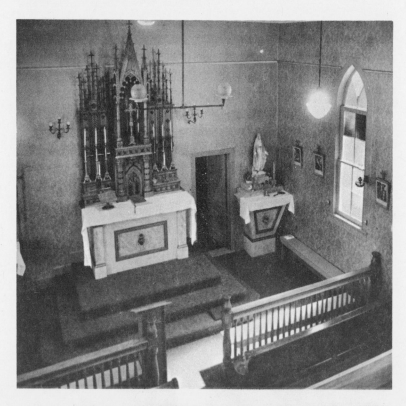

(Left) Fr. J.T. Fierens, first resident priest in Jacksonville. (Right) Fr. Francis Xavier Blanchet, nephew of the Archbishop, was appointed as second resident priest, stayed 25 years, saw strong Catholic membership develop, opened St. Mary's Academy for boys which was quickly closed—reopened for girls. (Lower) Fr. Blanchet in later years.

Fr. Francis Xavier Blanchet, priest in Jacksonville for 25 years, in the the church rose garden.
Same view for rose garden photograph, area in 1982. In mid-1930's garden was torn out to make way for Depression-era gold mines.

photographer Peter Britt sent his daughter as a boarding student to the Academy where the teaching was very strict. On one occasion, the students were quarantined during Christmas vacation because of measles. Miss Britt was determined to be with her family so she opened a window then slid down a balcony pole and went home. (The Academy was across the street from the Presbyterian Church.)

Fr. Blanchet (b. July 22, 1835 – d. May 22, 1906) was well-schooled and took his responsibilities most seriously. He did everything in his power to promote and advance Catholicism in Jacksonville. His masses were well attended. His homilies were often aimed at fund raising for church related projects, or levied against specific groups such as Masonic Orders. He was often gone from Jacksonville since his many missions extended as far north as Corvallis, to Empire on Coos Bay and to Lakeview. During his sometimes lengthy absences, it was not always possible to have an assistant or bring in a temporary priest, thus his flock was unattended.

Following the small-pox epidemic he became so ill from overwork that an emergency message was sent to a priest in Yreka to come to anoint Fr. Blanchet. This was done; fortunately he recovered. Fr. Blanchet was at St. Joseph's Parish for 25 years (1863-1888).

In 1875 he arranged to purchase the house which had become a rectory, on a sheriff's sale.

Mission stations supervised by Fr. Blanchet included Ashland (1875) and Medford (1890). In 1912 the church became a mission of Medford but closed in 1940. After sixteen years, it was reopened again as a mission of Medford. Although the little building seats only 103, the usual attendance for Sunday Mass in 1982 is reported to be about 125.

Over the next twelve years, according to official church records, nine priests were assigned to the parish. On July 10, 1889, the nuns operating St. Mary's Academy closed the school "because of a lack of 'spiritual succor,' the pastor often being on missionary trips for three weeks at a time." Also, the building was badly in need of repairs, which the Sisters were not able to make. Many people in Jacksonville signed a petition that the school might be reopened, but it was not to be until 1891. The Academy was moved to Medford in 1908, and at this writing operates as Sacred Heart School. For education beyond the elementary level, the Medford parish conducts St. Mary's High School. □

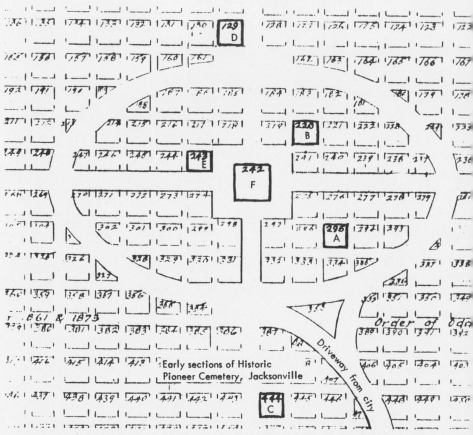

Center Loop of cemetery. A: Gabriel Plymale No. 295. B: Rev. Moses A. Williams No. 220. C: Beekman family plot No. 444. D: Britt family plot No. 129. E. T'Vault family plot No. 243 F: Sexton's shed.

Wm. G. T'Vault was an important personage in Oregon history. Before settling near Jacksonville at Dardenelles near the Rogue River, he was Editor of Oregon's first newspaper at Oregon City, and he was Postmaster General of Oregon Provisional Government. Dardenelles was the first Post Office in Jackson County opening on October 19, 1852. Regretably, no postmarks can be found today.
Monument marks site near Gold Hill exit, southbound Interstate 5.

38

CHAPTER 5

EPIDEMIC!

IN LATE 1869, AN ALARM RANG THROUGH THE VILLAGE WHEN A case of small-pox was detected. The first report indicated the case to be merely chicken-pox so by the time a corrected diagnosis was made, the case was full blown. Those attending the victim, a half-breed Indian, had freely circulated throughout the town. The genesis of an epidemic had been spread and it was not long before a death was announced. Although attempts were made to cloak the death in secrecy with the burial taking place at night, there were blunders and almost immediately additional cases were found.

A town-wide quarantine went into effect and word was spread throughout the valley telling all to stay away. Normal day-to-day activities in Jacksonville stopped. The school was closed and church services were canceled. All public gatherings were discontinued. Just south of town, a "pest house" was set up to which patients were taken and every possible care given. Despite the quarantine, two deaths were reported in one other locality.

In Jacksonville, the disease spread like a blanket and so did panic. Vaccinations were given. Even with this precautionary step, many seemed unable to relax. As Walling wrote:

> Ministers fled in affright from paths of duty, but in the darkest hours, the Catholic Priest [Fr. Blanchet] who himself had experienced the disease, together with the Catholic sisterhood, rendered valuable assistance. The contagion was not confined to any particular class. The widow of John Love, a lady of refinement and culture, was attacked and with her youngest son, was carried away. Her mother and the rest of her children were in the country and dared not approach her, and, when all was over, the unsightly corpse—all that remained of human beauty—was borne to the cemetery in a rough lumber-wagon, without a single follower.

William Green T'Vault, at 63, had led an active life in Oregon politics as well as being Oregon's first newspaper publisher (in Oregon City, 1846), died of small pox during this terrible epidemic. He was buried

(Top to bottom) Sexton's work shed built about 1868 and recently restored. Storage vault under floor in shed exhibited by sexton Wayne Maxon. Bodies were kept here before undertaking parlors had refrigeration. First burial in Jacksonville Cemetery was body of Gabriel Plymale in 1852. Many markers have been damaged by vandals. T'Vault monument is in block No. 243. (see map).

William Green T'Vault, first newspaper publisher in Oregon (1846), was also first newspaper publisher in Southern Oregon—Jacksonville (1855). T'Vault, a staunch politician, was apparent instigator in plot to force John Beeson, the single individual who stood for Indian rights, to flee the area for his life. T'Vault died of smallpox during the 1869 epidemic.

at midnight by Fr. Blanchet who had attended his dying moments. T'Vault had become a Catholic only a few weeks earlier. His many friends did not dare join the depressing walk up the hill to the cemetery. (T'Vault's grave and marker are just a few feet from the Sexton's shed.)

For about two months, the townspeople were in a state of confusion with death all around. Gradually the disease slackened, then wore itself out. Those who recovered would carry scars on their bodies for the rest of their lives. Jacksonville lost between forty and fifty of its people and in the small community their absence was notable.

One of the town's leading citizens, George Funk, died in a lonely cabin on the outskirts of town, cared for by members of the Odd Fellows Lodge. He was buried at the site as it was not considered wise to haul his body through town to the cemetery until some time later.

The people sought to end the pestilence by burning pitch pine in the streets, causing a layer of smoke to hang over the town to "purify the air." Such was the custom of the day. Clouds of smoke hung over the little town day and night, giving off a ruddy glow which lighted the streets. The smoky atmosphere didn't improve breathing and the so-called "cure" was not a cure at all.

The sisterhood from St. Joseph's Parish endeared themselves to the entire community of Jacksonville, having given tirelessly of their nursing skills to the many victims of the small-pox epidemic of 1869. □

Jeremiah Nunan house on Old Stage Road. This is remaining house of three ordered from a catalog and set up about 1890.

Benjamin F. Dowell house built 1859, still occupied as private residence, across from supermarket on N. 5th Street (Highway 238).

Table Rock Billiard Saloon constructed 1859, now antique shop.

CHAPTER 6

CHINESE

THE CHINESE WERE NEVER WELL RECEIVED IN MINING CAMPS, and the Jacksonville Chinese Community was no different. Drunken whites harassed Chinese merely because they were "different." Chinese miners worked harder and worked longer hours. They kept their gold to themselves and for their own projects and did not frequent the saloons. Jacksonville, really a shanty town of its own, did not cover a great area, so although the Chinese kept to their own "quarter," they were not that much removed from everybody else.

Lower wages for a day's work was the rule, thus many Chinese were hired by whites for the hard, or "coolie" work as it was called, denoting work done by one of a lower class.

Many white miners were sloppy with their work. When they believed a claim was playing out they abandoned the area and moved on. Chinese miners worked these same areas over and over again getting gold until there was absolutely none left.

Passenger lists reveal the Oregon Stage Company brought a steady stream of Chinese from California to work the Southern Oregon gold mines. The records of Jackson County Mining Claims shows that whites often sold their claims, which they believed to be worn out, to Chinese. Pressure was brought on the Territorial Legislature to tax Chinese engaged in mining. The tax license was $2 *per month*, and all able-bodied Chinese who resided or remained in any mining town were regarded by law as miners unless directly engaged in some other business. (Laws of Oregon Territory, 8th Session 1856-57 p. 13)

When the constitution of Oregon was being debated, an entry for September 15, 1857 reads:

> If Chinese emigration continued to come into [Jackson] County [it was] predicted that in five years no white man would inhabit it. White men could not compete with them—they work for $1.50 or $2.00 per day.
>
> —Carey, C.H. *The Oregon Constitution and Proceedings and Debates of the Constitutional Convention of 1857.* Salem. 1926 p. 361.

43

CHINAMEN

By Willia Isaacs

Gin Lin, wealthy Chinese miner
He employed many dozens of his countrymen in
his operations in the hills above Jacksonville.
Photo from Southern Oregon Historical Society

Chinamen are very patient and industrious. He digs, washes, irons, and does many other things. Chinamen live mostly on rice. Rice is the chief food in China. John Chinaman smokes opium in long-stemmed pipes. They have a room where they smoke it. Opium sometimes nearly kills them. They have flat noses, small eyes and a dark yellowish complexion. The women's feet are small and they go bare headed. Some Chinamen have long ques which are braided and hang down their backs.

In Article XV, Sec. 8, is the stipulation "No Chinaman [sic] not a resident of the state at the adoption of this constitution shall ever hold any real estate or mining claim or work any mining claim therein."

By the 1860's the Chinese were still working so-called worn out claims. Their numbers were greatly diminished, but those who remained were methodical. They only worked in areas where they truly suspected they would find gold, or where others had quit. If they hit a vein, they worked it until it ran out. In one instance, a group followed a minimal trail of gold by digging a ditch from Jacksonville all the way to a point near Gold Hill.

The only time the Chinese stepped out into the community was during the Chinese New Year. With the traditional Chinese Dragon leading a parade, these folks paraded in serpentine fashion around the town then back to their colony—with most of the town's kids bringing up the end. The children were treated to Chinese "goodies" and everyone enjoyed themselves. A few days later, when activity was "normal," the kids who had been treated one day, were throwing rocks at their hosts the next.

A very few Chinese stayed in the country after the gold ran out, then these too eventually drifted away. □

CHAPTER 7

THE U.S. HOTEL AND PRESIDENT HAYES

APLACE IN HISTORY WAS ASSURED THE UNITED STATES HOTEL when President and Mrs. Rutherford Birchard Hayes, and party, stayed overnight on the 27th of September 1880. A member of the party was General William Tecomseh Sherman. The story, with a variety of potpourri added for spice during the century following, is a good one to review here.

The building was not yet ready for guests but last-minute fixings were added in an effort to make the President's visit comfortable. The history of the hotel is notable because of the building's enduring nature and the love held for it by many Jacksonvillians.

A jolly but shrewd businesswoman, Madame Jeanne deReboam, operated a boarding house in town during gold rush days. Later, she had a place she called the "Franco-American," which was also a boarding house. One rented a room for a period of time — normally longer than merely overnight — with breakfast and supper included in the bill. Madame was an extraordinarily good cook and had no trouble keeping her place full.

George W. Holt (left), building contractor and owner of brick kiln, who built U.S. Hotel. Madame Jeanne de Roboam (right), "contracted" with Holt for the job—became Mrs. Holt.

The United States Hotel was constructed in 1880. President and Mrs. Rutherford B. Hayes, and party, stayed overnight here September 27, 1880, months before hotel was ready for occupancy. Upstairs gallery was officially known as "Holt's Hall," but later was just called the "ballroom." Beekman's Wells Fargo Express office at left.

Down the street was the United States Hotel, which pretty much catered to one-night visitors. After the U.S. Hotel burned in one of several downtown area fires, the lot was deserted. Through a former owner, Louis Horne, the Madame bought the lot. But she was confronted with a challenge: How to get a building on it?

There happened to be a skilled builder in town who also owned the brick kiln, George W. Holt. And there are some who believe the following as fact, others prefer to call it "spice" to make a good story. Anyway—it is told that a business deal was struck between "Jeanne-baby" and Holt whereby she would share his bed and provide his board for the rest of his life if he would build a brick hotel. Further, the deed must state the property would revert to her heirs on their deaths. (She had a son who wasn't known locally.) Holt agreed! They married of course, which was the fitting thing to do.

U.S. Hotel late 1880's. Organization on balcony possibly members of Order of Red Men from cross-sash ornamentation. It's said gatherings of this size on balcony caused balcony to weaken, collapse.

In March 1879 Holt went to work. That he was expert is attested by the fact the building still stands 100 years later. Though there were periods where severe renovation was needed, it's still in use. He designed the entire structure. He hired some outside workers but he also spent many hours in actual construction. There was no hurry to get the job done so Holt took well over one year with it.

For a dance on the 4th of July 1880, the upstairs ballroom was opened but the whole building was really not yet finished. It would be February of 1881 before Madame Holt (nee deRoboam) was ready for any renters.

When the President's party showed up in the fall of 1880, as we have seen, the building was unequipped and not ready for anyone to live in. The President's group was in two sections. The first passed through town without tarrying. The second group of eight was made up of the President

U.S. Hotel, it's sign and balcony gone appears foreforn and dilapidated in 1930's. Note fire plug which was installed about 1912 (top). Restored in mid-1960's, the U.S. Hotel is again one of the most attractive buildings in town in 1982 (bottom). (Next page) The U.S. Hotel behind wagon, viewed from lot on South 3rd Street, spring 1982.

and Mrs. Hayes; General Sherman; John W. Herron and wife; Mrs. John Mitchell; Dr. D.L. Huntington, all USA; (Col.) John Jameson. Haines wrote of "a woman newspaper correspondent" along but this was Laura Platt Mitchell—Mrs. John, a niece of the President and *not* a reporter.

The group arrived in the evening to a welcoming committee of a small group of Republicans. As the mayor was a Democrat, he could hardly be expected to be seen. (Oregon was one of four states where the

ballot had been contested. Hayes was declared winner by exactly one vote by a special election commission.)

The official greeting was a booming cannon and the brass band's appearance. As there was no advance warning of exactly when the group would arrive in town, all of the welcoming committee didn't make it. And of course, there had not been any earlier arrangements as to where this important party would spend the night. Madame Holt was located and implored to find a way to put up everybody in her new hotel. No rooms were ready. There was no furniture. Paint was fresh and sticky.

Recalling that the ballroom had been opened for the summer dance, it was dusted out and a reception and dinner was hastily planned. Even though it was already evening, the dinner would have to be stalled. The leading Republican, "Old Beek," turned out for the occasion and was pressed into being the welcoming speaker. In his book, Frank Haines wrote:

> This dinner featured Mrs. Hayes, known as 'Lemonade Lucy' for her prohibitionist activities. [She] turned her wine glass upside down as a

gesture of refusal. The ladies were so charmed by this genuine bit of Washington etiquette, that it became a local fashion.

The next morning the visitors were up early and left town in their 3-team stage coach before most of the town knew they were gone. All kinds of stories have evolved since that less-than-24-hour visit of a President of the United States to Jacksonville, Oregon.

Probably the most quoted unprovable anecdote has to do with the bill for $100 for the group's dinner and lodging. On eyeballing the bill, General Sherman is supposed to have retorted, "My dear lady, I did not intend to buy your hotel!" (But he paid the bill.) Another story goes that Mr. President complained about bedbugs. Bugs in borrowed bedding, especially in 1880 Jacksonville, could have happened.

The fact that a President stayed in the U.S. Hotel adds to the lore of the town although to this day no one knows which room he occupied and where ever the bed-bugged-bed was borrowed from does not seem to be recorded.

Years later the grand old building was ordered closed by the State Fire Marshall. He declared the hotel no longer safe. For one thing, the roof had been mended and re-covered so many times that its weight was about to collapse into the floor below. The town library had space in the hotel and was forced to move.

Interior, U.S. National Bank of Oregon, ground floor of U.S. Hotel, a full-service branch decorated in 1880 style.

North Side, California Street between 3rd and 4th Streets. U.S. Hotel (left), Ryan and Morgan Bldg. (right) now Jacksonville Inn, hotel and restaurant.

Eventually, the hotel was restored by activities of the Jacksonville Properties for Historic Preservation and the Lions Club. In summer, there have been special musical features of the Britt Music Festival in the ballroom.

The United States National Bank of Oregon's Jacksonville branch occupies part of the ground floor. The bank has taken great pains to furnish its office with fixtures fitting the early days. Many of the furnishings are authentic while some, needed to complete the office, are new but constructed to resemble original pieces. On some days, the bank employees dress in the costumes of the historical period. The bank's clock is an 1876 model located in Jacksonville and the green shades on the windows are true to the decor of early times. The roll-top desk near the Branch Manager's corner is 1860 period of oak and walnut.

In the lobby of the hotel is a glass showcase with relics of early banking. □

Peter Britt, Oregon's first photographer, arrived in Jacksonville in 1852. He brought his Daguerrotype camera, a Voightlander Serial No. 2115 and (in 1874) he was first to photograph Crater Lake.

CHAPTER 8

THE PHOTOGRAPHER

THERE IS LITTLE DOUBT THAT A LOCALITY WILL BE REMEMBERED in later years if, during its forming years, the town was lucky enough to have a nearby photographer. Jacksonville is unique in this respect for in the 1850's it was one of very few communities with a resident photographer.

Peter Britt was a Swiss who came to America sometime before 1845.

The Britt home and garden, daughter Mollie seated. Outline of Britt's home (below) as viewed in 1982. Now county park.

The family settled in Illinois. In 1852, with two others, Peter traveled to Portland then a frontier town. He was 33. He decided to head south with a yoke of oxen, a two-wheeled cart and a mule. He spent many days looking at the Willamette Valley but continued across the Calapooya Mountains into Southern Oregon. He came upon the gold mining village which was

53

becoming Jacksonville. It was the 9th of November 1852. The village was merely a bunch of tents and a few log cabins.

He had trained as an artist: a painter of portraits. But in St. Louis, before heading west, he studied daguerreotyping as he believed Americans would accept and pay for photographs more readily than painted portraits. Britt took up a claim under the Donation Land Act on a hill at the southwest corner of the village. His first task was to construct a log cabin which would serve as home and as a work place, for he had carefully carried a small, wooden box camera and developing materials from St. Louis.

In his first months in the shanty town he did little photography so in the spring of the next year, he went into the pack train business moving freight from the wharf in Crescent City to Jacksonville. He pursued this business until 1858. Britt wanted to make pictures full time but he needed more equipment and a source for supplies. He took a trip to San Francisco and brought everything he could think of with which to set up a formal studio.

On his return he added a second story to the cabin and installed a skylight. His darkrooms were upstairs. Britt photographed people as they were: Miners in rough clothing with pick and pan; Chinese he pictured in native dress; he did portraits of Indian maidens; soldiers; children; the businessmen of town; family groups. He liked the out-of-doors so photographed buildings, parades, mountains, flowers and streams. He was the first to photograph Crater lake (1874). When the National Park Superintendent learned of this, he made immediate inquiry about getting extra prints.

In 1860, he built the large two-story home which was a landmark for years. He added more rooms in 1880. He had other interests too. Having come from an area in Europe known for its fine wine grapes, he obtained starts from California and in a few years operated one of the first commercial wineries in Oregon. He put up Claret, Muscatel and Zinfandel which he distributed at wholesale.

Britt, a true believer in the value of catalog buying, ordered seeds and then planted many of the valley's first apple and pear trees.

When he was 42, he married a childhood sweetheart Amalia Grob who had been widowed with a small son. Peter and Amalia had three children of their own: Emil (1862); Arnold who died as a baby; and Amalia (1864).

To commemorate the occasion of the birth of his son, Britt planted a sequoia on the north edge of the property. It still stands. His wife watched

her husband's growing success but died in 1871 leaving him to rear the family.

Peter Britt loved his children and loved beautiful things. He worked hard to develop a garden around the house which included a fountain and a small pool. The property commands a view over the town and valley with the Cascade Mountains in the distance.

His son, starting at an early age, helped his dad in the studio. After Britt died in 1905 at age 86, his children, who never married, continued to live at the family home. They took great pains to preserve his work for he was an artist who had gone through life with seeing eyes, and had recorded what he saw with exacting and patient work. His great collection of glass plates illustrate the growth of the community both in buildings and people who lived there or passed that way.

Peter Britt was the first photographer in Oregon. His cameras and much of his equipment are displayed in the Jacksonville Museum where hundreds of his photographs are exhibited.

Peter Britt, his wife and their two children, are all buried in the family plot in the Jacksonville Cemetery.

Artist-photographer, Peter Bri[...]
lived to age 86, died in 1905. H[...]
accumulated very large runnin[...]
history of Southern Oregon in pi[...]
tures. In the Britt Room (belov[...]
of Museum. (Display subject t[...]
change.)

☆　　　　　　　☆　　　　　　　☆

Peter's property was originally some ninety acres. It was given to Southern Oregon State College with the understanding the house and antique furnishings would be cared for. A caretaker was hired to live in the house but, unfortunately, the house burned.

After the fire, the gardens were reclaimed with much volunteer labor until early in the 1970's, when efforts by members of the community persuaded the County to buy eleven acres which were the location of his barn, house, orchards and gardens. The $40,000 paid for these acres is used by Southern Oregon State College for loans to students. The money has turned over many times.

After securing the land, the Britt Assocation worked about eight years to obtain funds to build the present pavilion. The County financed the construction of restrooms. Donations from individuals and businesses along with a federal grant, enabled the construction of the pavilion.

The foundations of the Britt home were outlined and an attempt made to replace the gardens as they were when the home still stood, with a grant from Oregon's Bi-Centennial commission.

A path was built for pedestrians from the public parking area on Highway No. 238 behind the telephone exchange building.

The pavilion stands where the Britt barn stood years ago. The pavilion was designed then built to allow performers to project variations within a musical score to the hillside audience.

Irrigation, overhead lighting and access for the handicapped is being installed at this writing. Jackson County Parks Department assumes responsibility for the upkeep of the grounds. Each August, the Peter Britt Gardens Music and Art Association Festival presents summer concerts under the stars, on this original Donation Land Claim. □

Cornelius C. Beekman,
messenger, Agent for Wells
Fargo & Company, Banker,
Politician, Philanthropist.

CHAPTER 9

THE BANKER

NO NAME WAS BETTER KNOWN IN SOUTHERN OREGON BANKING circles than that of Cornelius C. Beekman and the Beekman Bank in Jacksonville.

He was a transplanted boy from New York City where he had been born on a very cold January 27th in 1828. He went to the common schools in the city and had trained as a carpenter. He was just 22 when he sailed to San Francisco via Panama then proceeded, with other gold seekers, to the Yreka area where he prospected for three years.

In 1853 he took a job with Cram, Rogers & Company a branch of Adams & Company express agents in San Francisco and Portland. He was regularly sent as messenger from Jacksonville over the lonely mountains to Crescent City carrying letters, papers and thousands of dollars in gold dust. In all the troubled times, the young fellow was never molested, although generally traveling alone and at night. In 1856 his employer went bankrupt and "Beek," as his friends called him, lost his job. Unperturbed, he went into the messenger business for himself, continuing the same routine. He rode at night, as mentioned, often changing the route. When a good stage toad was completed over the Siskiyous between Yreka and Jacksonville, he was in the right place at the right time, for Wells Fargo needed someone with experience to represent them at Jacksonville. Beekman accepted the post and kept it for many years.

In 1857 he opened a private bank which he operated with extreme conservatism. He bought gold dust at discount directly from miners, and transported it out of town. His profits were high and this venture guaranteed him a small fortune from the start. His bank was considered one of the richest banking houses in all the Northwest. For some years, after he took a partner, Thomas Reams, the bank was called "The Beekman and Reams Bank." When Reams died in 1900, Beekman continued alone. Of interest, is that Beekman didn't pay any interest on deposits, and when somebody wanted to borrow money, Beekman, if he approved of the loan, loaned his own money—never the bank's !

As a financier and man of considerable ability, he was repeatedly elected one of the town's trustees and for several terms was the elected Mayor of Jacksonville. For nine years he was President of the School Board and it was mainly through his efforts that the large brick school was built in 1908. His concern for educational advancement of the town's youngsters took a high priority in his life.

Beekman had interests in other fields as well. He was one of the founders of the Jackson County Land Association, that organization controlling large tracts of the county's land.

Of course a man of this ability would become involved in politics away from the homestead. We find Beekman, in 1878, being placed in nomination for Governor of Oregon on the Republican ticket. It was a wildly contested campaign and when the votes were in, Beek lost by only *forty-nine votes!*

59

The Beekman Bank (right) on California and 3rd Streets in 1982.

Beekman is reported to have had as a philosophy, "Let every man be occupied, and occupied in the highest employment of which his nature is capable, and die with the consciousness that he had done his best." — borrowed from Sydney Smith.

Beekman married Julia Hoffman, the daughter of the County Auditor. They had two children, Benjamin B., an attorney, and a daughter Caroline.

Beekman was, for twelve years, the Master of Warren Lodge No. 10, A.F.&.A.M.

As mentioned, Beek's bank was "different," in the manner it held people's money. "In reality," wrote Adam Richter in *A Century of Banking in the Rogue River Alley,* "Mr. Beekman directed a village safety deposit box and transported letters and other valuables. Moreover, he never charged anything for the bank's service."

He developed a fortune by loaning his own money and collecting a good interest, but never by oppressing the poor or by taking advantage of the necessities of his fellows. During his early business as a messenger, he carried letters for $1 each before the Post Office opened in Jackson County.

Beekman decided to close business after 55 years. On August 13, 1912, he told the public he wanted to retire and would pay off all depositors. Considering that The Beekman Bank was the pioneer bank in

Headstones for C.C. Beekman and for his wife Julia, in Beekman plot in Jacksonville Cemetery.

the County, this caused quite a stir. But "Old Beek" was getting along in years.

The retirement of the bank's business went forth with assertiveness, but Beekman did not live to see his institution finally closed. He died on February 22, 1915, at age 87. (Beekman, his wife and their children are all buried in the Jacksonville Cemetery.) The final closure was completed by May 1 of the same year.

Visitors to Jacksonville can view the banking office just as it was abandoned in 1915 at the corner of 3rd and California Streets. Under the control of the Southern Oregon Historical Society and the Jacksonville Museum, a large glass has been installed so viewers can see the office and its turn-of-the-century equipment from the street. In addition, there are two Beekman "houses," both on California Street. An early residence is on the northwest corner of 6th and California Streets and is known as the "Minerva Armstrong House." Mr. and Mrs. Beekman lived there right after their marriage. The second house, known as "The Beekman House," is a little east of the Presbyterian Church, on the south side of California Street. Both houses are museums and are maintained by the Historical Society. Both are open for visitors in summer and other times by arrangement.

☆   ☆   ☆

We do need to acknowledge that "Old Beek" had some competition in the banking business starting in 1907. The Bank of Jacksonville was capitalized at $25,000 and experienced a period of growth right from the start. Part, possibly, because not everyone in town liked to do business with Beekman. But about two years later, there was a sharp decline in deposits then a rapid recovery. This was followed in 1918 with another decline and the capital investment was reduced to only $10,000. Another binge of business brought the capital account to $15,000 but then trouble of a nature newspapers love to report came to light.

In short, the Bank of Jacksonville was ordered closed by the State Banking Department on August 11, 1920. In the trial which followed, several officers of the bank were found "wanting" as well as two customers. Four men were sent to the State Penitentiary for their parts in the mishandling of funds. The liquidation of the Bank of Jacksonville was one of the most expensive undertakings of the State Banking Department and required only three months short of ten years to complete.

> Considering the fact that this is the quietest month of the year in the banking business our banks have more than held their own with deposits. G.L. Davis of the bank of Jacksonville said that on the date of making the bank statement the deposits were smaller than they have ever been before. The next day the deposits jumped from $41,000 to 44,000. If the showing in the next six months equals that of the past six months which is quite probable, our financial institutions will show an increase to that of any bank in the state. The Beekman Banking House, one of the oldest in the state publishes its first statement, under the new law, in this issue of the POST. The stability of our banks is not questioned in the least, and are conducted along conservative and business lines.
>
> Clipping from Jacksonville Museum — date unknown

Of great concern was the fact that Jackson County Treasurer had deposited county funds in the bank in the due course of business. The loss to the county as a result of the bank's failure was about $107,000.

The Bank of Jacksonville's closure left the town without a bank until 1965, when the United States National Bank of Oregon opened its Jacksonville Branch in the U.S. Hotel Building. In 1976, the Jackson County Federal Savings and Loan Association constructed a building compatible with the neighborhood, on the corner of 4th and California Streets. ☐

CHAPTER 10

JACKSONVILLE WANTED A RAILROAD

THE MATTER OF HAVING A RAILROAD AS WELL AS A TELEGRAPH in the valley had been debated for years.

Plans for the telegraph line between Portland and Yreka went ahead after meetings in Jacksonville in October 1861. Fund raisers made the rounds in the spring of 1863, and work started shortly thereafter. The line was a tough job to install, but the first message was tapped out on January 23, 1864.

By 1863, the outlook for transcontinental rail service was quite promising so Jacksonville's promoters decided on a project that would bring a train through Jackson County. Subscriptions were accepted for money as well as merchandise to help with costs which would arise with a route survey. The first survey started in the Sacramento Valley near Marysville—at that time the northern terminal—and extended to the Oregon border. The plan also called for a railway to be built in Oregon to join with the California tracks. The funds collected didn't go very far but others stepped in for their piece of the action. By late summer 1864, the survey in Oregon was finished to the Columbia River and the results were put before the Oregon Legislature. Result: The California and Columbia River Railroad Company was incorporated. Joseph Gaston, a lawyer and journalist, envisioning a great future for the railroad, took an active part in a long and heated controversy over which route the rails would follow. While this delayed construction, Jacksonville continued to flouirsh as the principal city of Southern Oregon even though the miners had mostly moved on. After much turmoil in the courts over routes and grants, the Oregon and California Railway Company was awarded a contact. Work progressed up the Willamette Valley to Eugene where serious debates over routes were rekindled. Would the route miss the Rogue Valley by crossing the Willamette Pass and enter California through Klamath County? Or would the right-of-way pass through Roseburg and the Rogue Valley then over the Siskiyous to the state line?

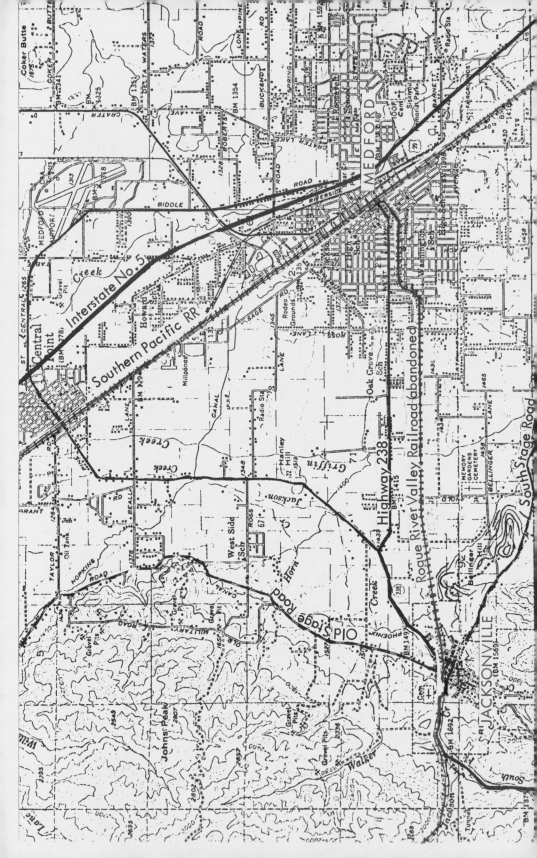

It was largely through the efforts of U.S. Senator George H. Williams (R-Oregon 1865-1871) that the route was decided in favor of the Rogue Valley. But the construction stopped at Roseburg without further progress for nearly ten years!

There was no question in anyone's mind that the tracks would pass through Jacksonville, for Jacksonville was the largest city in Southern Oregon. Several ideas were discussed in town to further the stalled construction, one of which was the formation of the Humboldt Branch Railroad. This venture, the planners believed, would construct the line through the valley. But the scheme died.

Finally, when the Central Pacific decided to build their line northward in the Sacramento Valley, work again commenced at Roseburg. The people followed progress of the work vividly. Word got out that the design engineers wanted to build in a straight line after the track crossed the Rogue River, to a point near Ashland. Still, Jacksonville businessmen and residents were of a common mind: "The rails will come through our town." When crews staked the line from Central Point to Phoenix, then Talent and on to Ashland, which would be the division point at the base of the mountains, Jacksonville boosters began to get the message that their town was going to be left right where it was—five miles west of the line!

A local group wanted to bribe the railroad so somebody passed the word that the town needed to donate a station and yard site and hand over $25,000 cash, and the track would be routed their way. Was it a sound idea? Did anyone have any money? Would Beekman's bank loan the money? Answers: No, no, and no!

When it comes to building a railroad, the matter of who owns the land it will run on must be considered. Some Jacksonville property owners had planned on making a killing when they sold rights-of-way for the tracks. At least one did, but as we will see it was not in Jacksonville!

One night, railroaders roomed in the village of Central Point. While there, the officials talked to villagers suggesting they put up money and land for switching tracks and a station. For some unrecorded reason, the proposition was not well accepted by the listeners. Folklore tells us that these locals told the money-hungry railroad men to "buzz off!"

In retaliation, the design engineers decided to build a new town just a few miles south thus drawing trade away from Central Point.

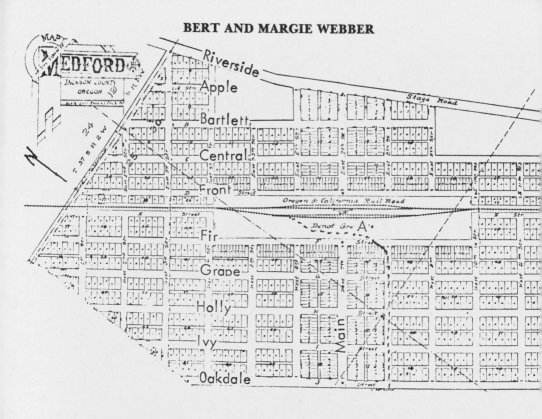

Original plat of Medford shows city "clustered" around Oregon & California Rail Road. Current street names superimposed along with route of R.R.V.R.R. tracks and ("A") Depot. Note city is aligned with tracks, not compass!

It happened that some farm land was owned by four men, one of whom was Beekman. They pooled their interests and platted a townsite. They donated 240 acres to the engineer in charge of the O. & C. survey, then donated an extra twenty acres to the railroad for a station and switching yards—plus every other block within the townsite. In all, the railroad received 41 city blocks. Many thought they saw a connection. Some believed that Beekman wouldn't loan money to bring the tracks to Jacksonville because if he did, he wouldn't be able to sell his land at trackside to the railroad. With a deal as good as this, why should a railroad detour its tracks via Jacksonville?

But there were other considerations that ruled out Jacksonville. There's certainly no question that the most economical route over which to lay tracks is in a straight line, especially when there are productive farms on both sides of that straight line. The O. & C. was running short on money. While it would be polite to Jacksonville to jog the tracks in that direction, Jacksonville had no economic base from which to generate freight. In addition, the entire line from the Rogue River was up-grade all the way to the California line, so why huff and puff by way of Jacksonville when there was no business to be gained? Thus, observers have noted, the railroad never seriously planned to pass through Jacksonville all the way back to the earliest planning stages.

Storekeepers in Jacksonville were getting nervous about construction at the new town. Some told customers the buildings were merely warehouses to transfer goods from the railroad to "J'ville". After all, Jacksonville *is* the county seat and as such, *is* the center of county operations! The new court house would be built the next year and that alone meant stability—they truly believed!

Meanwhile, and very quietly, some merchants prepared to move to the new town. Medford, as the town was to be called, was founded—or platted—during December 1883. It was a little over one year later, February 24, 1885 to be exact, when Governor Z.F. Moody signed the bill incorporating the City of Medford. On March 11 of the same year, the articles of incorporation were adopted locally.

Jacksonville began to feel it was slipping further when word first got out that the railroad would miss the town. Many shook their heads in wonder as to their future as Medford, that upstart railroad town to the east, became a reality. But "li'l old 'J'ville' " would survive as a one-industry town—the county seat—another 44 years. When the politicians started to promote the removal of the county seat to Medford in the 1920's, Jacksonville's future took on the look of a freight train roaring down hill with no brakes.

Even though the Oregon and California Railroad would never touch Jacksonville, interests in town wanted a railroad so much, they put their possibility thinking together and decided to build one of their own. Feelings ran high that with a short line to Medford, freight and passengers by rail would keep Jacksonville alive. It was a fight for survival in the minds of many, as Medford was growing like an unwelcome weed. Ashland, never before of much concern to Jacksonvillians because of the distance, suddenly seemed much closer. It was the division point on the O. & C. Railroad folks were swelling the town whose population now topped Jacksonville's. In addition, there was an uncomfortable situation developing just six miles northeast: Central Point had nearly doubled in size and straddled the rails.

(Central Point got its name because two pioneer wagon roads intersected there—which is near the center of the valley.) Meetings were held and often became heated as committees pondered how to get, and where to seek a right-of-way between Jacksonville and Medford. A railroad would have to hire people for construction as well as for operation and this meant money would flow to Jacksonville, they reasoned. With this spark, even Medford became involved. People in both towns pledged a bonus of $20,000 to get a railroad out of the planning stages and into reality. The first official effort was the incorporation of the Medford and Jacksonville Railway Company in mid-January 1890. This operation was to choose depot sites and prepare final surveys. There was a deadline just less than one year away. A train had to actually operate on the line if the bonus was to be paid. There was lots of pressure to get track down. But it is one thing to envision an operating system on paper and another to order, receive and install ties and rails, buy an engine and cars, have everything shipped and get a train to run. Time waits for no one. With less than a month before the construction contract expired, rails had not been delivered let alone nailed down. The contractor left the job. To believe such a project could have been completed within the time allotted seems, with advantages of 20-20 hindsight, to have been ill-conceived. There are no records available today for anyone to review as to source or rail specification. There is good reason to believe however, that a hardware store in Portland, which specialized in heavy metals, got the order. This dealer took delivery on second-hand, 36-pound rails which had come from England.

A new contractor was appointed and work progressed rapidly with new enthusiasm. What had been a job noted for delays, now went ahead with amazing speed. Final grading was completed just as S.P. told the builders that a full train of flat cars carrying rail was due on the morrow.

Rails were nailed to ties in record time.

Fully aware that they had no rolling stock, the contractor borrowed or leased an engine and car from Union Pacific. (As there was still ill-feeling against the mainline firm for not routing their tracks via Jacksonville, why rent from them? It was now the Southern Pacific to be reckoned with as O. & C. had gone bankrupt while trying to get over the Siskiyous.

The deadline of January 1, 1891, was at hand. It was a very cold, rainy day. There was no ballast (rock) yet poured to weight the ties in the

Picture is believed to be arrival of the little 10-ton Porter locomotive and the passenger car at the Southern Pacific yard in Medford in 1891.

soft, wet earth. The U.P. engine made steam and barely started to roll when the tracks slipped and the engineer found his mount parked firmly in the mud! The engine was far too heavy for 36-pound rail on non-ballasted ties.

Jacksonville's people were not dismayed for long. They were pleased with the progress of their contractor so granted a construction extension. About two weeks later, folks suddenly froze in their activities as a sudden shriek split the air—a train whistle—as the first train hissed and chugged its way into town to the site where the depot had not yet been built. There was a celebration that day to rival the 4th-of-July!

The new line was greeted with enthusiasm both by Medfordites and Jacksonvillians. Just about everyone wanted to ride the train although regular service was not yet available. All trips were being done with borrowed equipment as the ordered engine and cars still hadn't arrived. Nevertheless, groups chartered the train for special trips. It was announced that the ride to Medford was only twenty minutes. There was concern, in official circles, about the west-bound trip to Jacksonville which took longer. It was a steady uphill pull; not that the grade was overly steep or mountainous as some writers would have readers believe. The Medford

Everybody wanted to ride the train! Rogue River Valley Rail Road ran between Jacksonville and Medford, about 5 miles.

Bench Marker reads 1,383 feet altitude and Jacksonville's 1,569. This is only 186 feet in five miles and hardly noticeable to the eye, except for a trifling increase for a very short distance at the Jacksonville city limit near the school. Nevertheless, it costs more fuel to puff a train up any grade than when a train goes down grade.

It was pointed out that the O. & C. went broke trying to complete their line over the Siskiyou Mountains. It will interest some to learn that from Ashland to Siskiyou summit by straight line is about 9½ miles. By the track, 17 miles. The grade commences immediately on leaving Ashland but increases to 3.3 percent—reportedly the steepest on the entire S.P. system—near the summit at which point a train, with helpers required, has climbed about 2,178 feet altitude.

The Union Pacific engine was returned with the arrival of Locomotive No. 1, a Porter, 10-ton engine. And with its arrival also came a challenge. The little engine, which is said to have been designed for the near-flat surface to the New York elevated railroads, was severely underpowered for pulling a train up the slight grade into Jacksonville. There was no choice but to find another engine.

70

The new short line received the U.S. Mail contract between its two terminals. Editorials in the Jacksonville *Democrat Times* envisioned a connection to the coast and a line to Eagle Point thence into Central Oregon and of course, transcontinental.

About one month after the tracks were finished, a new corporation was formed for the purpose of operating a railroad between the two towns and for two miles beyond.

We recall there was a brick kiln west of town. Brick is heavy. The manufacturers looked to selling their output not only in Jacksonville but elsewhere, so it didn't take much persuasion for the railroad to put in a spur to the plant. Up Jackson Creek a ways was plenty of rock which could be used for ballast, hence the plan to run the tracks two miles beyond town. These were days when if rock was needed from the side of a hill or from a creek or river bottom it was mostly for the taking—no "permits" required!

But all this construction would be costly. Capital stock of $100,000 to be split into 1,000 shares was offered and bought by investors. The company

A second locomotive was purchased when the little Porter proved too light for the job. Here the train, with combination mail-baggage/passenger car in rear, instead of behind tender which is normal, waits on "C" Street facing west just over the Depot switch. Note Court House tower and flag to orient direction.

Tracks of the **Rogue River Valley Rail Road** extended about two miles west of town up Jackson Canyon to rock quary. When line was electrified in 1915, this west end extension was abandoned as the steam engines had been sold.

took the name Rogue River Valley Railway Company (even though it operated from a point — Medford — on Bear Creek), and began regular service on Lincoln's birthday, February 12, 1891.

There would be two round trips each day. Jacksonville's depot was constructed at the corner of N. Oregon and "C" Streets. (Renovated a few years ago, it now serves as the Chamber of Commerce Information Office.)

Southern Pacific would earn extra profits if their loaded freight cars were used an extra few days. Instead of having to unload a car in Medford, only to be reloaded on a car of the shortline, it was suggested and agreed that a switch between the two firms' lanes be installed. S.P. henceforth would just park a car with Jacksonville-bound freight on a siding then the local engine would hook up for the final leg of the haul. As it meant faster service for "J'ville" customers, the deal was approved.

In April of 1891 the contractors declared their work finished. The line was formally inspected and accepted and Jacksonville's people were happy

A Trip to Jacksonville
By Grace Davis

I went to Jacksonville on a swift passenger train which has just commenced running lately. The train is a combination of an engine and one passenger coach, and sometimes a freight car.

On my way to Jacksonville I saw a great many things of interest, green fields and pastures, farms, houses, orchards and some very beautiful flowers.

Some of the people I saw were very good looking, and others were not. I also saw some Chinamen but they were not any different looking than they are here, because they all look alike. I went around the city awhile and then to the court house to hear a speech after which I got my dinner at a restaurant. I saw the jail, many large stores and several nice dwellings. For my part I like Medford the best of the two towns for the reasons that it is a larger place and is on the main railroad.

The Jacksonville-Medford jerk water met with the usual delay Thursday night, only this was more usual, when the engineer-fireman-brakeman-president-machinist conductor-section boss-office-boy-official started out with a gallon of water, and a few sticks of wood and a broken injector to make the round trip to Medford, he found that the S. P. passenger from Portland was late and there was not sufficient water in the boiler to make the round trip and wait on a late S. P. train, but nevertheless the start was attempted from Medford. After traveling about a mile the engineer noticed that the water was very low in the boiler and attempted to start the injector, but the old faithful injector worked as it has oft done before (worked the engineer.)

The engine was backed down, by gravity, to a residence, the fire pulled and the boiler filled by buckets. By this time the boiler was cold and several long minutes passed before the steam was raised. When the beautiful iron horse and palace car entered the city another unexcusable stop was made in front of the court house, and there the Rogue River Fast Mail stopped for the night—for want of steam. Several passengers became disgusted with the thing and walked to this city.

Clipping courtesy Jacksonville Museum—date unknown

---

with the news, for at last they had their railroad.

Although many speeches were made and lots of meetings held, promoters were never successful in extending the line to Eagle Point.

The stockholders, who turned out to be more interested in construction than in mere day-to-day operations, leased the railroad in October 1893 to W.S. Barnum who lived in Medford. Barnum was to operate the line for two months—just until the end of the year. Probably the most newsworthy item about this lease was that Barnum's 14-year-old son became what the press heralded as the youngest railroad conductor in the country.

The 1893 panic hurt plans for any expansion, even additional cars, as new investors could not be found. Ownership changed several times

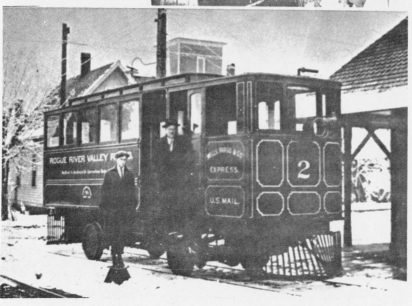

General Offices of The R.R.V.R.R. Company in Jacksonville (top). This gasoline-engine-powered single unit was built in Oakland, California. It was cheaper to operate than a steam train which was never filled with passengers. But riders didn't like the new "train-car" many complaining it "jerked, squeeked" and made them "seasick."

Gasoline-powered covered "speeder" used for quick trip charters. Old timers who remember the ride said it had "no springs, hard seats, hard on the 'sitter,' creaked, but was a lot of fun to ride."

resulting in the construction firm which had finished the work having to operate it. The line was never profitable. The haul was too short and there was only one recognized stop enroute, Perrydale Avenue, about midway between the two terminals. There never was any freight for Perrydale, just a quick passenger stop. What freight was hauled went west, up the fuel-consuming grade into Jacksonville. The train generally went to Medford — down grade — empty of revenue producing freight. Jacksonville, as county seat, needed the passenger service. There were "commuters" so the railroad sold monthly booklets of "commute tickets," each ride rated 20 cents.

As there was little provision for maintenance, the cars as well as the roadbed deteriorated which forced frequent shutdowns.

Both nature and people play tricks on railroads. The operation was, of necessity, low budgeted. When the engineer got a good head of steam up in Medford for the run west, he tried not to pile any more wood into the fire box than was absolutely necessary to get the train into Jacksonville. If there was a stop at Perrydale Avenue, this took most of the reserve steam to get the outfit rolling again.

The train, on entering Jacksonille over that "trifle" of a grade near the school, frequently met with delays because boys would be boys! The rascals sometimes greased the tracks then disappeared into the building to watch the engine's wheels spin on slick iron. The train would lose its momentum—stop. The engineer would appear shortly with a bucket of sand which he spread on the tracks so the wheels would regain traction. There were occasions when cattle occupied the tracks stopping the train once putting the engine in the shop following an encounter with a steer.

The cwners, based in Portland, tired of the novelty of railroad ownership which didn't bring any profits, wanted out. Barnum, who had run the line for a couple of months earlier, bought the entire works for a reported sum of only $12,000.

Under Barnum's ownership, the road became mostly a family operation as his wife and several sons took jobs. He hired few outsiders except for firemen. This "Mom and Pop" operation saw Mrs. Barnum as secretary, treasurer and business manager. The boys worked in the shop, handled what track repairs were required to keep the train on them and of course, one son was conductor. Dad was General Manager.

The Barnums' did their best to run the venture as a profit-making business but without substantial freight and with dwindling passengers—automobiles had arrived—the future was not bright. Jacksonville was definitely not growing. In fact, it was the other way around. Medford quickly surpassed Jacksonville in population and in business houses. The orchard industry, apples and pears mostly, was centered in the valley and "J'ville" was miles away. People silently blamed all of the town's troubles on Southern Pacific for the "shortsightedness" in skipping Jacksonville. And shame! There was the beginning of talk about moving the county seat.

Barnum's life was never easy. He was charged with blocking traffic in Medford by leaving his train unattended for hours. Others contended the coach was unsafe and they had to resort to umbrellas on rainy days as the roof leaked. And the car creaked over the now uneven road bed.

When the all-surface road between Medford and Jacksonville opened, a jitney carried passengers for less fare than the railroad. Barnum was a fighter—he cut fares. It was expensive fighting. Barnum purchased a train-car; a combination freight and passenger unit powered with a gasoline engine. People charged that the thing "stunk, jerked" as it rolled along the track, and was not at all what they wanted! Their dreams would never be realized.

Another challenge irked Barnum when in 1913, the Southern Oregon Traction Company formed for the purpose of installing electric interurban lines throughout the valley. Not that any such new transportation was needed, but that was the plan. Barnum saw a way out of his headaches, so in 1915 he sold out to the interurban people for part cash and part mortgage *held by Barnum!* And here is where Barnum was shrewd. He really liked owning and running a railroad but he was out of cash. If he could sell out for a good sum of hard money but hold the papers on a railroad which was a proven loser, he'd get a rest, then eventually get the line back.

Of course the first thing Southern Oregon Traction did was shut down the railroad and electrify it. Jacksonvillians believed this electrified

---

TELEPHONES IN JACKSONVILLE

Exactly when the first phones were used in Jacksonville is elusive. A writer in 1878 declared it "undignified" to talk to an invisible listener," but in the same month people could talk on "wires" to Yreka.

The 1899 telephone directory listed four subscribers in Jacksonville. These were: Line No. 12   George Hines Boarding House

No. 13   T.J. Kinney Hardware and Grocery Store

No. 14   S.P. Roboam, United States Hotel

No. 15   John S. Miller, Hardware

In Medford, there were 16 lines.

The Pacific States Telephone Company, which operated the toll line between San Francisco and Portland, wanted more revenue and this meant more subscribers to telephone service. A manager arrived to talk with the gentlemen in Medford, who kept the switchboard in the rear of his store about getting more business.

It will be noted that Jacksonville was the county seat but, according to that 1899 phone book, there were no phones in the Court House!

The Medford switchboard attendant curtly told the fellow from San Francisco that the first priority for business increase was to get rid of the toll costs between Medford and the county seat. This was promptly attended to and phone installations in Jacksonville increased sharply. In 1982, Pacific Northwest Bell Telephone company reports 1,933 phones in the Jacksonville 899- prefix area.

In 1915 the line was electrified. Pictured is curve in city of Medford near present corner of Columbus and 11th Streets, facing southwest. Trolley wire not yet hung. Man unidentified.

This "Cleveland-built" streetcar (below) was purchased from Portland's street railway system for use on the now-electrified R.R.V.R.R. which had become Southern Oregon Traction Company. This only known photograph shows car abandoned and vandalized on siding in Jacksonville.

line would be the end of their problems with the railroad. It cost considerably less to run an overhead trolley car than to generate steam every time a train had to move. A car was bought in Portland from the transit system there and hauled to Medord on a flatcar. But "mass transit" developers failed to recognize the potential drain from their enterprise by automobiles which were increasing in surprising numbers. The cost of electrification was never recovered. In short order, as Barnum expected, the interurban people wanted out. Barnum got his line back in default but grossly improved. A few years later Barnum sold it again. Same deal: Cash, and mortgage which he held. He got it back again.

Somewhere along the years, not pertinent to this story, tracks were laid in Medford streets for local streetcar service. A rare photo shows Barnum's steam engine and work car in the middle of a down town Medford street with crews digging up the street a few feet in front of the locomotive, laying ties and rails, then the work train proceeding a few more feet where the operations were repeated.

Medford had streetcar service for a short time but it, too, ran into money problems. And some people complained about having to change cars from east Medford to the car that ran on the Jacksonville line. With all kinds of problems, some with the "Cleveland" car itself, a connecting switch was installed between the two companies' tracks. For awhile, the "Brill" car on the Medford line offered through service to Jacksonville. Every time some new sort of improvement was announced, Jacksonville's people cheered!

It all came crashing down when the power station serving the line burned.

It was now summer, 1922. A couple of years later, when another prospective buyer came to town, a special hookup was made from the local power company for a demonstration ride from Medford to Jacksonville and return. This must have been quite a ride! The rails were overgrown with weeds and the corroded trolley wire shot sparks. Because the track had settled, the few passengers received a swaying, seasick ride. The deal fell through.

In 1925 Barnum decided to pull up the tracks and sell out for scrap. But law suits stopped his tearing up city streets. Finally in 1925, the City of Medford, which very much wanted to rid its streets of the rusted rails, bought the entire line to the Jacksonville city limits and sold a lot of the

M. Dale Newton, railroad historian a[nd]
map maker, at restored Jacksonvi[lle]
Depot of R.R.V.R.R. (top), spri[ng]
1982. Newton shows two 4-inch spik[es]
(bottom) from R.R.V.R.R. found [in]
1982 by historian Novus Webb [in]
Jackson Canyon. Newton kneels [by]
exposed length of original track on "C[?]
Street just east of 5th near southw[est]
corner of museum. Of several lengths [of]
track under asphalt pavement, th[is]
alone remains exposed—may be cover[ed]
during next street improvement proje[ct.]

Many street sign posts in Medford are old rails from R.R.V.R.R., according to M. Dale Newton, railroad historian.

parts for salvage. But Medford did not sell all the rails! In 1982 one can drive through the streets in southwest Medford, in the area where the tracks were, and one will still see tracks—but not in their usual position! Several dozens of corner street name signs are held aloft on the ends of sections of railroad track which now serve as poles.

In Jacksonville, the track was mostly left in the pavement from near the depot on "C" Street to 5th Street at the southwest corner of the museum. The track was asphalted over but in the 1970's a thin layer of the pavement had worn off one rail exposing it to view. "Ah, ha" exclaimed historians! But will the city cover it with street improvement projects in future?

The little locomotive, old No. 1, rusty and abandoned, went to a logging operation near Cottage Grove, Oregon, where it hauled trains of logs on reasonably flat land. Still later, abandoned again, it was purchased by a woman as a gift to her husband who was a steam locomotive enthusiast. The engine was shipped to California on a flatbed truck where it was totally restored. □

81

The City Hall was built on the lot where earlier had been the first brick building in Jacksonville. That building burned in 1874. The present use of the old City Hall is for Municipal Court and public meetings.

CHAPTER 11

SCHOOLS, FIRES AND SCHOOLS

WHENEVER PEOPLE GATHER INTO A NEW TOWN WITH children, it isn't long before steps are taken to start a school. We have seen that Emma Royal, whose father was an early Methodist minister, conducted school for a month in the winter of 1853. Her effort was well received so she was hired the following year by the newly formed Public School District. The first terms were necessarily short ones. In April 1855, the school directors picked a site for a building on North Oregon Street. It took nearly two years of tax levies ($550 each) to build a frame schoolhouse and pay the teacher. The second Rogue Indian War (1855-56), coupled with other community interests resulted in interrupted school schedules. There was no compulsary education at this time so attendance could not be enforced. Teachers needed to have other income-earning capacity, and frequently let their contracts drop if a better job came along.

Jacksonville was a staunch pro-slavery stronghold and many of its substantial citizens would hear of no compromise. Without compulsary school attendance and some reported pressures to teach pro-slavery platform, a proper school environment was to be delayed several years. In fact, by 1860 any semblance of a "working" school system seems to have completely disappeared. It was during the Civil War that Fr. Blanchet decided he would promote the establishment of a school which would admit young ladies to a general curriculum with a Roman Catholic flavor. The town's population was growing and schools were sought. The public school was not functioning thus, say some, Fr. Blanchet's idea was well received. As we have seen, St. Mary's Academy opened its doors.

There is little doubt that the success of the Catholic school brought pressure to bear on the long inactive public school board. The trustees met and decided it was time to start anew with a new school building. As might be expected, opposition to school expansion was great from citizens whose own education was deficient, but who, through good fortune, had taxable property. In time, well-wishers won, property was acquired then a building erected. Regretably, there were to be many unsettled years for education in Jacksonville as partisan politics crept into almost every issue. A hill on the northeast edge of town, Bigham's Knoll and some seven acres adjoining, was purchased in 1868. $600 was raised, with Beekman's help, to construct a two-story frame building. A Jacksonville builder and cabinet maker was awarded the construction contract. Cost over-runs are not of recent invention for an additional $1,000 was needed to complete the work.

When the building was finished, most of the town turned out to look at their new school. The Board decided that a school year would run six months. Two teachers were hired to serve 79 boys and 46 girls.

But how does a school marm notify the town that classes are about to begin without a bell? "Old Beek," as the town's then only banker was called (but never to his face), raised the cost of a bell by sponsoring a formal dance and minstrel show in the ballroom of the U.S. Hotel.

Jacksonville's school district experienced several tragedys with its buildings. When the new school burned to the ground just three years after being opened, the patrons stood together and built a larger one. The 125 students of three years earlier would grow, as it was believed there were close to 350 children of school age in the area. Of course St. Mary's would siphon off some, but as there was no compulsory education in Oregon until 1889, some parents didn't send their children to any schools. The Board decided to build a four room school to be staffed by four teachers. While a county school office did exist and taxes were levied, collecting taxes was a continuing problem. Regretably, few Jacksonville teachers lasted more than three years and neither did the principals.

At one time a School Board ruled that teachers who drank liquor would be dismissed forthwith.

During the small-pox epidemic of 1869, the school closed its doors.

Teachers who enforced discipline sooner or later had some parents to contend with. Tales got home about happenings at school but seldom did a parent hear both sides of an issue. Regretably, then as now, parents who complained of their child being disciplined at school were all too frequently the parents who did not discipline their children at home. Very often the good kids were kept in along with the bad kids. This caused certain parents to stomp up to the school as their child had to suffer because of the rowdiness and troublemaking of others. But how was a teacher to handle it? In the 1872-73 year there were 85 students with only a

84

Jacksonville's first brick school (above) built in 1903, lasted only two years—burned 1905. It was replaced immediately with another brick building (below) which opened in 1908. This picture is 1918.

85

husband/wife team as educators. These two were also disciplinarians, tenders of the school yard, ringers of the bell, fight breakeruppers, as well as writers and editors of reports for the School Board. Then as now, there was always a group of people who were against schools, said so vocally, and voted against budgets.

Most pre-teen boys, attending school near the turn of the century, felt uncomfortable and out of place when ordered to sit still at a desk in a room with *girls*. Instead of studying, these fellows would much rather be catching toads and taunting girls. These were days before school counselor-pyschologists, thus teachers generally ruled the unruly with force. Any kid who was out of order was marched off to the principal's office—often dragged there by an ear! Nearly all of these boys had their knuckles banged with a ruler many times and the really unruly could be whipped. It was not uncommon for teachers—many of whom must surely have earned their high blood pressure trying to "teach" pre-teen boys—to leave the room then sneak in the back door specifically to catch the room clown in a prank, grab him, then shake him until his teeth rattled or until teacher was out of breath, then slam the kid down in his seat!

No wonder Vance "Pinto" Colvig and his chums cheered when the school burned in 1903, for this meant no more classes at least for awhile. Was the town, and later the country, ready for this boy who could turn the school and the town inside out with his irreverence and shenanigans—a boy with no feeling for conservative traditions?

The ashes were barely cool when work started on the new building. This one, of brick, would go up in record time.

A miscellaneous problem had bothered teachers and kids alike, especially girls. Wandering cows, sometimes prodded into the building by Tom Sawyer-type boys and left there over weekends with dire results on the floor, had to be fenced out. The School Board ordered a picket fence around the grounds with a narrow gate at the base of the hill. But there seemed no way to keep the gate on its hangers on Halloween!

In the yard, girls were assigned to one side and boys on the other. No one dared cross the imaginary line even to chase a ball, for there was a teacher-monitor always there during recess with a handbell. Any boy who ventured into the girls' side brought forth a vigorous shaking of that bell and the possibility of a whack from the principal.

At first, water was hauled to the school each morning in a tank-wagon which was parked near the front door. After unhitching from the wagon, the driver walked the horse back into town. Early in a recess, boys would frequently pull the plug causing a rapid evacuation of the tank. This caused 1) a muddy puddle right near the front door, 2) girls couldn't get back into the building without soiling their shoes, 3) teachers became very angry, 4) of course no one would squeal as to who did it. Eventually the Board got tired of this prank so they dug a well on which they placed a hand pump.

At recess, girls jumped rope, played drop the handkerchief, tag. The boys liked sliding in the mud from the draining tank. Boys played marbles—which teachers confiscated at every opportunity, spun tops—which teachers confiscated at every opportunity, and played "king in the tree." The first boy up the tree at recess was "king." The object of the other boys was to haul him down, cracked head or not.

A new sport was sweeping the country—roller skating. When the basement was finished in concrete, the girls were allowed to skate there during recess. Research does not indicate if the boys had skates or if they did, where they skated.

Of course these school buildings did not have inside plumbing—just privies near the fence. There was one for girls at the side of their yard, farthest from the boys. The Board put the boys' privy on the opposite side of their yard away from the girls. These privies were well bolted down as the Board was well-on to the boys' tricks—they thought. Each was a three-holer. These toilets were pretty crude by today's standards for a "pit" or "vault" field toilet. These were just holes dug in the ground. They were never cleaned, stunk, and were noted for flies. Of earth-shattering magnitude one day was the discovery, in the girls' privy, of a hornet's nest under the seat! In the spring, it was not uncommon for the girls to dash for the privy at recess only to find the door missing! (During an interview for this book, the author learned of a one-time-only escapade where, over a weekend, some boys completely filled the girls' privy with dirt.)

Mornings, as the 9 o'clock bell clanged, everyone dashed for his exact place in line before the main door. Once in place and all was deathly quiet, the two lines, one of boys, one of girls, marched to the tapping of a hand bell up steps into rooms where each pupil stood in a brace beside his or her desk. At a signal, each room recited the Pledge to the flag. Then the teacher ordered all into their seats. It was the very same every morning except one. On this day, classes were just being called to order when a boy shot to his feet and pointed to a flame in the new brick building. Children were hustled outdoors as smoke thickened, and the volunteer fire department was summoned by one who ran all the way to the station and jerked on the bell rope. Although the firemen responded, nothing could be done to save the building. So great were the flames, they were reported seen as far as Eagle Point.

The brick school had been the pride of the community. Its loss was great as the insurance was for only $10,000. To replace the structure would be twice that much at least.

When school opened in fall 1906, classes were scattered all over town. The Presbyterian Church basement was used as was the town hall, the newspaper office and the second floor of the brewery. It was not until late January 1908 that the new building was ready.

Newspaper accounts claimed the brand new building was one of the handsomest and best appointed in the state. The building was nearly 100 feet long with a 56 foot frontage. Advertised as "absolutely fireproof," it was heated by a steam boiler. Classrooms were 32x25 feet and illuminated by electric lights. There was a library and special "teachers' room." For use in bad weather, the 3,600 square-foot basement was designed as a play room. The general assembly room had a stage fitted with footlights. As the original bell was lost in the fire, a new 500-pound bell was ordered. On Fridays, the school band played a concert from the cupola. Probably the most appreciated feature was "inside" plumbing!

The first world war brought profound changes to Jacksonville. There were many of German decent who had been residents for years. The town newspaper, the *Post*, was anti-war. There was no industry in town so many men, who were not drafted, left to work elsewhere. Of the departing men, some were teachers. With a teacher shortage some classes were combined. But probably the most severe impact on the schools was bickering within the School Board. Principals and teachers became "tools' of some Board members with some teachers being fired in plays for power. The high school could not open one year because of a shortage of teachers from this in-fighting. The School Board was left with no choice but to make a deal with Medford on a tuition basis. An inter-city jitney was hired to carry Jacksonville's students to Medford's high school.

Time was marching by with little impact on Jacksonville. A notable occurance however, was the building of the first "gas" station in 1914. The newspaper wrote that having a drive-in station would lessen the fire hazard as cans of gasoline, filled in the back rooms of stores with a hand pump fitted to a barrel, would be discontinued.

One of the frustrations of the town was to see its youth leave as there were few employment opportunities in the home town. Teenagers began to see "the other side" when they were whisked to Medford for high school. Medford had a real train which brought interesting people to town. There was a "movie house" which was officially "off limits" to the commuting students, but they read the advertisements.

In the beginning, Jacksonville's school was pure basic academics. If there were any "sports," it was of the after school variety. In the early 1920's, under pressure, the District rented the upstairs ballroom at the U.S. Hotel for a basketball court. The school got its own gym in 1924. Following the opening of the gymnasium, organized sports became a part of the curriculum.

Spankings for boys' infractions gave way to manual labor. The Principal supervised boys equipped with picks and shovels to excavate an

This 1915 post card is labeled "Main Street" however view is looking east on California Street from Oregon Street.

The 1908 building is scheduled to close at end of spring 1982 term to be replaced with a new building a few blocks away. Disposition of the old building or the property awaits Board action.

area which would eventually become a basement next to the gym.

In one era, with many vacant houses, the county moved the poor to Jacksonville as a mean of housing them cheaply. Traditionally the poor do not vote favorably for school budgets. With funds short, the building maintenance was cut to a minimum which resulted in a need for almost constant repairs.

Real estate values declined and so did taxes. At one point, teachers were paid with warrants as the District had run out of money.

The Superintendent surveyed the District patrons and reported to the School Board the majority favored consolidation with Medford. Thus, the election of 1959 favored termination of classes above the 6th grade. The town had earlier lost its high school. Now it lost its juniors. As the old building further deteriorated, the cupola was removed, and later the second floor was closed to occupancy.

Many old timers in town did not favor the consolidation with the Medford District and vented their frustration with "no" votes at annual levy balloting. (Some still do!)

Nevertheless, the Medford School District No. 549C decided the 1908 building had served long enough and must be replaced. In spring 1982, work started on a new elementary building which is expected to see its first classes sometime in 1983.

Throughout this book have been many mentions about Jacksonville's two brick schools atop Bigham's Knoll—indeed landmarks. At this writing, no decision had been made regarding disposition on the 1908 building once the new school is opened. □

CHAPTER 12

"PINTO"

A S MENTIONED EARLIER, THE SCHOOL HAD ITS RUN OF CLOWNS especially in spring when boys' thoughts wandered easily from text books. It would take Jacksonville quite a number of years to realize that one of the nation's best known clowns had grown up in its midst. Vance DeBar "Pinto" Colvig was born in Jacksonville in 1892. He was the cut-up of the town and earned the name "pinto—the village clown" at the age of 7, because of his crop of freckles and goony antics. (The family home still stands at Fir and S. Oregon Streets.) His father, Judge Colvig, took him to Portland to the Lewis & Clark Exposition in 1905, but "Pinto didn't get any farther than a side show on the Midway. He saw a guy beating a drum to get attention for his show, so he went up to him and ventured, "I can play a squeaky Clarinet!" The man told him to come back on the morrow, but the boy dashed back to the hotel, got his E-flat Clarinet then raced back to the stand. He was put to work right then. The following day when he arrived, the man put "clown white" on his face, gave him a hat and dressed him in oversize clothing. He became "Bozo-the-Clown" that day and used that title for the rest of his life.

Colvig later wrote, "I guess I was just meant to be a clown." As he grew up, he learned to draw cartoons and was quite expert by the time he reached 6th grade. "Pinto" wrote many years later, "A cartoonist is just a clown with a pencil!"

Colvig loved the circus and ran off to join the A.G. Barnes Circus. In school he would squirm through winter sessions but come spring he'd hit the road. He went cross country riding the rails and had many a meal with hobos along the tracks.

Pinto was always ready to put on a show with his squeaky Clarinet and clown outfit. He entered Oregon Agricultural college (now Oregon State University) and played E-flat Clarinet in the Cadet Band. His objective? He didn't know if he wanted to become a professional clown, a musician, a writer, or what. He stayed at the college only three years. Later, he took a

Vance "Pinto," "Bozo-the-Clown" Colvig in the front row (2nd from right) about 1904 in first brick school. Of this picture Colvig declared years later, "At the time photo was taken I was either half-asleep; wasn't interested—or possibly drawing pictures in one of my books. The art work on the blackboard is mine; but definitely *not* the arithmetic, I assure you!" Colvig in typical clown outfit (right).

position in Nevada on a newspaper as a political cartoonist, then he moved to San Francisco *Bulletin*. Finally in 1922, he and his wife moved to Hollywood where he became a comedian and writer.

"Pinto" did some work for Walt Disney in 1930 then he held a contract with Disney Studio in the mid-1930's. During that period he worked on "Snow White and the Seven Dwarfs" as the voices of "Grumpy" and "Sleepy." In the Mickey Mouse series, he was "Pluto's" voice and that of "Goofy." In the animated movie, "The Three Little Pigs," his voice was heard as the "Practical Pig." His musicianship came in handy and his ability to write lyrics brought him fame and great royalties with the words to the hit tune, "Who's Afraid of the Big Bad Wolf?"

During the height of his "Bozo-the-Clown" popularity, one could buy "Bozo" coloring books, record albums, dolls and other toys.

On the radio, he did sound effects for Jack Benny's famous Maxwell automobile which never ran smoothly but "huffed, snorted, wheezed" every time "Mr. Benny" drove it.

"Pinto" Colvig never forgot his home town, Jacksonville, although his work took him elsewhere. The clipping file in the library of the Museum reveals he visited town numerous times in later years. Durng a 1963 visit he was a Marshall in the summer parade.

A theatrical agent once listed him as good in "offbeat characters, clowns, creeps," and mentioned that Colvig had hosted three award-winning childrens' series, and acknowledged that he was a professional musician—"E-flat Clarinet."

But kid's records in the old 78 rpm don't last forever. In 1982, while preparing this book, the authors asked listeners on Medford radio station KMED for donations of "Bozo-the-Clown" books and records for the Children's Department of the Jackson County Library. There was no response.

Vance DeBar "Pinto," "Bozo-the-Clown" Colvig died at age 75 in 1967. Mementos of his life's clowning can be viewed and appreciated in the Jacksonville Museum. □

Judge C.M. Thomas sentenced the DeAutremont brothers to life imprisonment from this desk in this room which is preserved within the Jacksonville Museum.

CHAPTER 13

THE LAST TRAIL

JACKSONVILLE HAD ITS SHARE OF "POLICE ACTIONS" STARTING with the murder of a gold miner in the very early days. Later, a very popular sheriff was killed in a shootout with a young desperado at the edge of town. There were numerous clashes with the Ku Klux Klan. And there were little things as when the town cop had to chase boys off the tracks when they were caught greasing the rails. In addition, there were the usual cases which fill a court docket day in and day out.

But the most notorious crime of its day to be committed in Jackson

Jackson County Court House was scene of famous DeAutrement trial in 1927. Deputy Sheriff Lewis Jennings (right) escorts Roy DeAutremont into Court House for trial.

County occured in 1923 when the DeAutremont brothers held up a Southern Pacific train in a tunnel high in the Siskiyous. The brothers dynamited the mail car seeking money which they believed was on board. They didn't get a dime! But they killed the Railway Mail Clerk — a federal offense, and the trainmen. Although the area around the tunnel (No. 13) and the tracks were thoroughly searched, there was no trace of the fugitives. It would be several years before the brothers were captured. One had joined the U.S. Army and was in the Philippine Islands. He was caught because a fellow soldier recognized his picture on one of the 2,583,000 "WANTED" posters. It was announced that the trial would be in the Jackson County Courthouse. The town was immediately in the nation's headlines as the trial got under way in 1927. Then the other two were apprehended in Ohio, also because of the posters.

The town filled with reporters and spectators and for the first time in years, all the rooms in the U.S. Hotel were rented. The trial was heated as arguments went back and forth, but in the end the DeAutremont brothers were escorted to the State Penitentiary at Salem for life. (For many pictures and details of the holdup, see the author's book, *Oregon's Great Train Holdup*, Ye Galleon Press.)

One of the brothers was parolled in 1950, but died of cancer shortly thereafter. Another was freed in 1972 and at this writing is still living. The third was transfered to the State Hospital because of mental breakdown.

The trial of the DeAutremonts was the last major event to stage in the Court House. Medford had been agitating to become the county seat for several years and a hot campaign had been waged in 1927. Following an election, the Medford people found themselves winners by a landslide. Quaint little "J'ville" did not have enough people to swing the vote. The fine Court House in Jacksonville was vacated when the County built a new one in Medford. Eventually, the building became the permanent home of the Jacksonville Museum.

With the loss of the county seat, Jacksonville lost even more businesses, especially lawyers. Lawyers traditionally like to have their offices in the shadow of the courts. (They don't have to walk so far in rainy weather.)

Medford developed rapidly. It became Southern Oregon's leading bruise on the landscape and greatest polluter of the once clean air.

With the financial crash of 1929, many wondered how much Jacksonville's economy would sink? There was no commerce, no factories to close. The railroad had ceased and even most of the track was gone. People were without jobs everywhere and "For Rent" and "For Sale" signs appeared all over the little town. The town was just plain tired out. It just seemed to want to rest after all the hassles and failures to retain its once greatness. Jacksonville just went to sleep and would remain in a state of hibernation for four decades.

The depression had hit hard. People who had homes in town began to think of the historic past. Some put their possiblity thinking to work realizing the town might be sitting on gold. Gold? *GOLD!* □

CHAPTER 14

WHERE THE STREETS ARE LINED WITH GOLD

WITH MEN OUT OF WORK AND NOTHING ELSE TO DO, some turned to digging for gold in their back yards. While some old timers had a little mining experience, most of the folks did not. Holes were dug anyway and the dirt was carefully washed. Sharp eyes scrutinized the pan looking for sparkles of gold dust. If none, or little was found, holes went deeper — many becoming shafts straight to bed rock maybe twenty feet down. Some of these shafts were four to six feet wide while others were no more than man-hole size. As the dirt was hoisted out, it was washed with water hauled from the house. A few made enough money to keep their families off the relief rolls.

A number became adventurous. Once down their shafts, they started to tunnel under the rest of the yard then under their houses. There was little risk of cave ins as the hardpan above the tunnels would support a lot of weight. Some shafts and tunnels were lined with timbers by the more progressive men, and on a few operations, sheds were constructed over the shaft to ward off the rain.

But the back-yard mining didn't necessarily stop at property lines. A.C. Van Galder went down through his back yard near a tree and then tunneled almost to the old railroad station. His tunnel was reported to have been about four feet high and twelve feet wide. (In the winter of 1980, a parked pickup truck's front end crashed through the city street near the telephone pole immediately west of the old train depot. Many believe this was one of Van's tunnels.)

But Van Galder didn't stop with one hole. He dug another in his yard but it was "dry." No gold. Earlier, a fellow had dug at the corner of the property and this was also dry. They filled the hole with old rock and bricks then planted a redwood tree in the middle. Today one can see the tree still nicely growing on the east side of North Oregon Street just north of "C" Street.

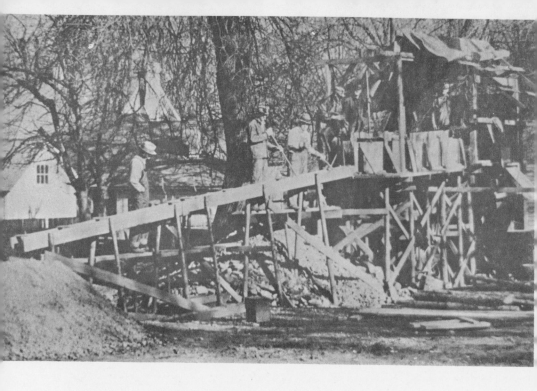

There were dozens of mine shafts sunk in back yards and in vacant lots where some fellows took out enough gold to buy groceries, others struck it rich but many got nothing. This is A.C. VanGalder's backyard operation on "C" Street just east of Oregon Street, where he and partner did very well. Another VanGalder operation (below) at corner of 4th and California Streets. He and partner Jack Green sank shafts in what is now service station lot, did extensive tunneling, took out much gold.

Partnerships for back yard mining were common, because to make progress it took two or more men. One partnership sank a shaft in a yard then tunneled under California Street at 4th Street. The digging continued under the building for another forty feet. A fellow who had been a City Mining Inspector, Wes Hartman, told the author when he notified the partners of his pending inspection, they found reason to delay him — while they boarded up lateral tunnels he didn't know about.

Then there was the mine under California Street near 5th, with "headquarters" where the present corner service station is located. In the center of town there is another service station (at 4th Street). This whole lot was once a storage yard for mining equipment and was the site of another major mine shaft. Van Galder and Jack Green dug up an estimated $25,000 in gold there. It has been rumored through the years that Jacksonville passed a City Ordinance prohibiting mining in the City Limits, however no trace of such an Ordinance can be found today, according to personnel in the City's offices. Anyway, who'd want to stop a little friendly back yard digging?

In the 1852 gold rush, Chinese laborers were plentiful, and there was a "Chinatown" area in Jacksonville. In the 1930's, some tunnelers rumored they had hit old Chinese tunnels but found no gold. Small wonder. The Chinese, if these were indeed Chinese tunnels, were very thorough in their very quiet mining operations and never knowingly left any of the precious metal behind them.

Just east of the Presbyterian Church was another mining operation which was the subject of complaints. A housewife pleaded to the town Marshall that she heard strange noises, "scratchings" and sometimes "grunts" under her house in the middle of the night. These noises turned out to be miners Bill Kennedy and Henry Dimmer. When their tunnel reached the area near the east wall of the church, they quit.

One father-and-son team reported years later that between $20,000 and $30,000 in gold was taken from their backyard and understreet ventures in about seven years.

Several enterprising fellows set up sluice boxes on Daisy Creek at positions in the city. One was located on "C" Street where the creek passes under the street near 7th. Another was located on Daisy Creek below the school near 8th and "E" Streets.

In 1933, under a New Deal project, Medford's school Superintendent

PARTNERSHIP AGREEMENT

THIS AGREEMENT made this twenty-sixth day of July, nineteen hundred and thirty five, between Joseph E.McIntyre, Leonard Osborn, Frank Taylor, and George Campbell all of the City of Jacksonville, State of Oregon.

WITNESSETH, as follows

I. That the said parties abovenamed agree to become partners in mining operations of J.S.Sawyer and Joseph E.McIntyre in Jacksonville, Oregon.

2. This agreement shall be effective for ninety days from the above date.

3. The said parties above named agree to pay to J.S.Sawyer and Joseph M.McIntyre 20% of all gold as royalty.

4. The said parties, Joseph E.McIntyre, Leonard Osborn, Frank Taylor and George Campbell agree to share equally the remaining 80% of all gold taken from this mine, after the operating expenses have been deducted from the same.

5. The said parties agree to cease operations should J.S.Sawyer and Joseph E.McIntyre desire to sell the property.

6. The said parties agree to hold J.S.Sawyer and Joseph E.McIntyre harmless from any and all claims, demands, and suits for damages or injuries received in said mining operations.

7. The parties agree to cease operations is J.S. Sawyer objects, or any controversy arrises from mining under the street.

8. The said parties agree not to mine within under the residence of J.E.McIntyre or anklength closer to said residence than I2 feet surface distance.

9. The said parties agso agree that no equipment shall be purchased unless all the said parties agree to the purchase.

Frank Taylor

Leonard Osborn

Geo Campbell

C + 8th St.

Godward Mercantile Co.

Godward's store bought gold dust and paid off in groceries or in cash. Receipt to Fred Christean who with Bill Dobbyn operated on Forest Creek in partnership.

was asked to provide three-day courses in effective gold mining for the benefit of the people who wanted to try their luck and hopefuly stay off the scanty relief list.

Two miners were contracted to teach the classes. Two days were in the classroom and the third day was a field exercise. The course was short and precise. Included were these topics:

> How to care for the gold pan
> How to pan for gold
> How to trace and locate placer gold
> How to trace and locate quartz gold
> How to build and operate a sluice box
> How to build and operate a rocker
> How to file a valid location of a claim

A third man was hired as "field man" to travel the area and assist miners as he found them. One of his tasks was to help miners with

Following World War II, Bill Dobbyn (top) and Fred Christean formed another partnership. With a drag line dredge operating in Jackson Creek just west of Oregon Street, they brought in over $1,000 per week on some weeks. Report on bullion shipment (below) for April 22, 1946, gave partners $1,217.48 to split after expenses.

negotiating royalty agreements with property owners. Most of Jacksonville's back yard miners were operating on their own property, so those who attended the classes were basically new-comers to the art of gold mining, who panned for gold elsewhere.

While the depression lasted, many of the unemployed spent most of their time working in their backyard mines. The gold dust extracted was generally sent to the United States Mint in San Francisco. As it wasn't practical for miners to take the gold there, they sold at discount to a handler. In Jacksonville, one middleman was the Godward Mercantile

Company, a general store. (If one wanted to reach the store in 1938 by phone, just ask "Central" for No. 74) Bill Dobbyn and Fred Christean had a mining partnership called Forest Creek Placer Mine. They often dealt with Godward. On March 5th, 1938, for example, Fred took in 1 oz. 13P-16 gr and was paid $47.95. Three days later he returned with more dust valued at $81.95 but the proprietor didn't have the cash so he receipted for the gold with the notation, "Pay next time." Bill Dobbyn told one interviewer years later that Godward would pay higher prices if the miner brought in several ounces at one time, rather than smaller amounts frequently.

Dobbyn and Christean decided to set up a dredge in Jackson Creek late in 1941, and were just getting started when the Japanese attacked Pearl Harbor (Dec. 7). They operated for a range of about 200-yards from N. Oregon Street upstream to a point where bed rock appeared on the surface. Dobbyn told the author that they bought the old wood-bottomed dredge, which was about 20 x 30 feet in size, in California. It was hauled to Jacksonville then reassembled at the site. Very little gold dredging was done however as the War Production Board shut off all non-military-essential materials. Steel cable was the major item of shortage, thus they shut down and engaged in other pursuits during the war.

After the war, materials were again available so they returned to Jackson Creek. Their dredge was fit with a 1-yard capacity bucket. They moved around considerably within the confines of the area, working upstream to the left of the present creekbed, then back down. The course of the creek was changed as the dredge moved slowly along as it took lots of water to operate. Dobbyn emphasized however, that the project was not intended to be a year-around job, as Jackson Creek traditionally dries up any time after mid-June.

Some examples of Dobbyn and Christean's labors are reflected in the following receipts for gold dust sent to the United States Mint in San Francisco.

On April 17, 1946, Bill Dobbyn carried dust to the U.S. National Bank branch in Medford, for which a teller receipted for 40 oz - 19 PW -14 gr gold-amalgum for shipment to the mint. The bank advanced $1,230 allowing $30/Fine ounce against what the government would pay.

On April 22, the Mint issued a "BULLION DEPOSIT – MEMO REPORT" in favor of the United States National Bank of Oregon (Deposit No. 1608)

Dry-land dredge working field on former Wendt property east of Jacksonville 1946-1948. The Jacksonville Mining Company dug up hundreds of tons of earth, recovered a lot of gold but expenses denied the operators much profit.

as follows:

DEPOSITOR: C. & D. Mining Company.

MINE: Jackson Creek (Oregon)

DESCRIPTION: Grains & amalgum

ASSAY no. 2101

WEIGHT BEFORE MELT: 40.97

WEIGHT AFTER MELT: 39.85

ASSAY CERTIFICATE FINENESS: Gold .874-¾ Silver .014-¼

BREAKDOWN OF FEES:	Melting:	$1.00
	Refining:	$1.59
	Handling:	$3.05
	Total Chg:	$5.64

VALUES: Gold $1,220.03   Silver $3.09

TOTAL (Less Charges): $1,217.48

Wesley Hartman, former City Mining Inspector, points to area for Bert Webber, research photojournalist, where sidewalk and curb sank years later due to tunnel dug during depression days mining venture. Area is on south side of California Street just west of 4th Street.

From this the U.S. National Bank deducted $2.08 advanced to Railway Express to move the original amalgum to San Francisco, plus the bank's handling charge (profit) $1.20.

Dobbyn and Christean realized $1,214.20 from this single shipment, which they split 50-50 between them. Dobbyn recalls their usual routine was to carry gold dust to the bank about once a week.

On May 23, 1946, these fellows received another "BULLION DE-POSIT—MEMO REPORT" from the mint for 51.814 FINE ounces of gold and 6.94 FINE ounces of silver. Their proceeds on this shipment were $1,805.60. On this shipment the breakdown of their amalgum shows: .880 gold; .118 silver; .002 base metals as copper, lead, etc.

When Jackson Creek dried up, the fellows pulled the dredge out and sold it. They set to getting a newer, metal-bottomed dredge which they worked on Foots Creek at some miles distant from Jacksonville. The area chosen didn't do well enough so they gave up gold mining.

During the early 1930's, Dobbyn said he had worked areas other than Jackson Creek and had some luck. "I didn't get rich but I made a decent

Patrons in Jubilee Club Restaurant on October 14, 1982 saw pavement "dip" under passing car then cave in when a heavy truck passed over a few minutes later. By another hour, the street collapsed, as shown, into an old gold mine cavern which had been excavated from a shaft on northwest corner of 4th and California Streets in the 1930's. Photo courtesy Scott DeMuesy, *Medford Mail Tribune* Right: Researcher Bert Webber entered "mine" through the street cave-in as Steve DeKorte (far right) of Jacksonville Public Works Department stood "guard." Webber, a 6-footer, is standing on caved-in earth about 10 feet above floor of cavern which was on bedrock. There is about 3 feet between top of Webber's head and street level.

living," he told the author. Bill Dobbyn winces just a little when talking (in 1982) about his venture saying, "Man—wouldn't I like to have all that gold back today and sell it at current prices. I got $30/ounce then and it's $300/ounce now!"

☆   ☆   ☆

With the advent of the second world war, many of the back yard shafts were filled in, but it appears nobody bothered to stuff the tunnels. Years later, a lady drove her car into the carport of her home when suddenly the front wheels sank and the car rested on the frame.

When Mike Moore was driving one of the city's fire trucks on a routine inspection mission and stopped at the corner of 5th and "C" Streets for the stop sign, the street under one of the rear wheels suddenly collapsed. A Van Galder tunnel?

The sidewalk and curb on the south side of California Street sank several inches without notice. This is just west of 4th. It was here that a tunnel ran under the street from a shaft on a lot where the Jackson County Savings and Loan office now stands.

Probably the last recognized mining occurred in 1957 when city

workers were digging for footing sites for the new Jackson Creek Emil Britt Bridge on N. Oregon Street. The city agreed to dump the mud into pickup trucks if persons interested would be at the site when the shovel was working. Several loads went into the pickups to be dumped in backyards where the dirt was washed for gold at leisure.

In 1932, the Chamber of Commerce developed a scheme to bring people and money to town. Why not hold a "Gold Rush Jubilee"? People were deeply hurt by the depression and needed to release tensions by having a rip-roaring old-time celebration. The event was apparently well handled and made some money. The next year plans were refined and an even grander affair was staged. To gain a degree of mirth, the Jacksonville *Miner* insisted that the streets would be thoroughly swept to remove excess gold nuggets and "rotten quartz" left by miners as they strolled through town. The mayor admonished:

> If the dogs in town would do their digging on the flats or in the back yards instead of in the city streets...there wouldn't be all this gold lying around for people to stumble over. Yesterday the Marshall reported that Emil Britt's Cocker Spaniel got out of the yard and started to bury a bone in front of Charlie Chitwood's place, and rolled a big hunk of gold down the hill as big as your hat. Roy Smith came driving along and nearly busted a wheel on it. Such business has to stop or people will be afraid to come to the celebration.

Why the annual jubilee didn't continue in the next few years is unknown, unless the power behind the event was someone who tired of having all the responsibility.

Last "mining" in Jacksonville was in 1957 when city crews scooped out mud for footings of Emil Britt Bridge on Oregon Street over Jackson Creek.

Nearly twenty years later, boosters in Jacksonville wanted to bring back the jubilee, so in 1950 there was a big push to do this. It was an eventful year, as the old Court House had been officially recognized as the new and permanent home of the Southern Oregon Historical Society's Museum. The museum had occupied the building earlier, but now it was to be official. A dedication was part of the program. The town was beginning to move ahead again. The following year it was staged again, and attracted wide attention when the National Broadcasting Company moved in with a production team to make a 30-minute feature radio program based on local history. But it looked as if Jacksonville had again shot its wad, for subsequent years saw a falling off of enthusiasm for the annual event. 1956 was the last year.

A contributing factor to the failure of a Jubilee was undoubtedly that the celebration lacked a theme. As Oregon celebrated its Centennial in 1959, the event was revived, but lack of enthusiasm was obvious and the "celebration" did not leave the home folks feeling the results were worth the effort.

In recent years, the Jacksonville Volunteer Fire Department has sponsored a "Pioneer Days" in June. This seems appropriate as the down town district is truly a scene from the past and is recognized as a National Historic Landmark.

At last the celebration has a theme. □

CHAPTER 15

LATER...

IN THE LATE 1930'S, WAR THREATS IN EUROPE WERE HEARD IN America. Men were called to work in war related industry and some, in the Oregon National Guard, were called to active duty. Jacksonville was again seeing its men leaving town. But suddenly, high wage work appeared in the country as the Army announced plans to build a camp in an area typical of Army camp locations — in the middle of the Agate Desert northeast of Central Point. The desert was nearly as flat as a pool table, grew desert-like flora, and was inhabited by field mice, jack rabbits and some rattlesnakes. Camp White became its name. The construction called for a central power and heating plant which required lots of ditch digging for the "conduit" which would carry the pipes and wires. The camp would include a huge Army hospital and a recruit training area. The cantonment would need lots of water and sewer lines. There would be a gunnery range. All of this meant jobs. It also meant that vacant houses in Jacksonville would be filled with workers imported from other areas, as well as for many Army Officers some bringing families. And it all happened.

The camp later became a P.O.W. center for German prisoners, some of whom, after the war, came back to make the Rogue Valley their permanent homes. Camp White became White City, Oregon, and in 1980 gained its own postal ZIP code — 97503. Industry had leased much space in what became Medford Industrial Park. Thousands of persons built homes, or hauled in mobile units on the fringes of the once arid Agate Desert. The former Army hospital was converted to become the major Veterans Administration Domiciliary in the United States.

☆　　　　　　☆　　　　　　☆

Various motion picture producers over the years have visited Jacksonville and the surrounding hills then came back to make films. The most recent major filming was "The Great Northfield Minnesota Raid" in late 1970. The movie people arranged a deal with the city to work over

Pioneer Day Festival in 1982 was sponsored by the Jacksonville Volunteer Fire Department which entered several units. (Top) The 1883 pumper, which was retired in 1912 and is on permanent exhibit in the Museum, was pulled along the parade route by (left to right) Bob Gemaehlich, John Stagg, Dale Smith, Don Laibe, Russ McIntyre (chief), and Dale Staib. During a fire, the pumper would be rushed to the scene, and a hose cart (not shown) would lay hose between a cistern and the pumper. There were three cisterns in town; one each in front of U.S. Hotel, Catholic Church, Court House. When the city built a reservoir on Jackson Creek in 1911 and installed fire plugs in 1912, the pumper was no longer needed—retired. A Ford "T" light truck was used to haul hose in the 1920's but was replaced by a 6-cylinder Chevrolet pickup truck in 1931. (Below) One of several powerful fire trucks in the Volunteer Fire Department in 1982 includes this Ford manned by (left to right) Joe Stagg, Sam Gemaehlich, Ralph Hubbard and Mike Vladeff, who rode the unit in the 1982 parade.

110

some of the historic buildings that didn't have an "historic-enough" look. They covered the paved street with dirt and placed wooden sidewalks over concrete to add authenticity. Hundreds were hired as "extras" to appear in the picture. It was a great time of re-living the past and everyone loved it, especially when the movie was released and many flocked to a theatre to see themselves on the screen.

When it was all over, some lamented the ripping up of the "temporary" wooden sidewalks.

☆   ☆   ☆

When a small town, whose buildings are primarily frame, had a fire, it was frequently a major conflagration. The great fire of 1873 roared through much of the town and took out Louis Horn's United States Hotel.

Then there were what became to be called "merchant" fires where a brick store building would be gutted—all the insured stock destroyed. Volunteer firemen are great guys and do their best but in days when mere hose carts and bucket brigades were the only equipment and methods, little headway was possible on a major fire. In an effort to stop town-destroying fires, the town council passed an ordinance requiring all new construction in the business blocks to be of stone or brick. Even so, over the years there were major fires that destroyed business buildings, and some home fires forced occupants into the night saving only what was on their backs.

Jacksonville's fire fighters used a hand pumper in the early days but retired it when hydrants were installed on the city streets in 1912. Fully motorized "fire trucks" would not appear for quite some years nevertheless, the volunteers always met at regular intervals for training sessions and practices right from the first. Today the firemen are still volunteers and some are merchants whose shops are close to the Fire House. The Department is part of the mutual assistance plan where it gives help to other localities if called upon, and in turn can call for help from other departments. □

CHAPTER 16

IT'S HISTORY IS IT'S INDUSTRY

MANY PERSONS WANTED TO KEEP JACKSONVILLE A SMALL town with close ties to a great historic past. Others wanted to develop the area for general residential construction as well as for condominiums, plus a huge shopping mall to be surrounded by an asphalt jungle. There were, and still are, quite a number who don't care what happens. But for the vigilance of a few, the old town might have been leveled long ago.

With very few exceptions in American history, towns developed along

Built in 1883, the Jackson County Court House became the official home of the Southern Oregon Historical Society's Jacksonville Museum in 1950.

One of the few Indians in town. He has to come in at night—he's wooden and can be seen in front of the Jacksonville Exchange on 4th Street.

some kind of a thoroughfare. The first trail through what was to become Jacksonville, became known as the main street along which businesses sprang up. As the town grew, more "streets" were added. A surveyor platted the town in the late summer of 1852 and the main thoroughfare became "B" Street—later California Street.

That main artery carried in its day: walkers, horses and riders, wagons, stage coaches, then automobiles. Also: light trucks, heavy trucks, autofreight trucks, loaded logging trucks, gasoline tankers, campers, vans, trailers, etc. Early in the 1960's, the State Highway people planned to reroute Highway 238 and bypass the town. There were several empty, rickety frame houses in the northwest part of town, not in the core historic area, whose values were pretty low. Any one of them would topple with a mere nudge of a bulldozer.

The route would take off from the present highway in the vicinity of Blackstone Alley and North 5th Street, take out those few old buildings staying south of Jackson Creek, pass west of the historic Rogue River Valley Railway Depot then rejoin the highway on California Street near the present city shops. This would keep through-traffic out of the center of the historic town. It would not be a high-speed route as the city would set the allowable speeds. There were people in town who thought this might be a good plan, but others didn't like it. True, the historic core would not be touched, but, so reasoning went, to tear down historic buildings on the periphery would detract from the whole.

Arguments see-sawed back and forth. The mayor, E.O. "Curley" Graham, sought an appointment with the late Glen Jackson, head of the State Highway Department. As mayor of Jacksonville, the appointment was readily given. Graham took with him Robertson "Robbie" Collins, an expert in community preservation and a resident of Jacksonville. They talked with Jackson as well as with then Governor Mark Hatfield. The State didn't want to listen—they'd already prepared the plans for the bypass. Shortly thereafter, when "Robbie" was in the east, he talked about the matter with several people including the late Senator Wayne Morse.

Much later after he'd returned home, so "Robbie" points out, word reached him that an assignment editor for *Life Magazine* had learned something about a highway about to be built that would squash a quaint little historic village in Oregon. The editor called Glen Jackson. The editor verified that such a road construction project was indeed in the works. Of course Mr. Editor didn't know everything about the issues but it sounded like a sensational story that *Life* might want. The editor is reported to have declared that he'd send a team and a cameraman to photograph Jackson sitting on the front of the first bulldozer taking the first bite out of the town! That killed it.

Traffic still (1982) plods its way through the main streets of Jacksonville—loaded logging trucks, auto-freighters, gasoline tankers, Winnebagos, tourists, bicyclists and pedestrians. Are there other potential

Constant attention must be given to the preservation of historic buildings. The Methodist Church gets a new foundation in spring 1982.

The bronze plaque is at the corner of 3rd and California Streets at the Beekman Bank.

bypass routes available? Surely, but they cost money and the State Highway folks may be a little shy of "J'ville."

But another highway project would aid in the awakening of Jacksonville.

The marvels of road building were realized in Southern Oregon when Interstate (freeway) No. 5 was designed then built more-or-less right through the middle of Bear Creek Valley. To the south, it climbed the Siskiyous with graceful curves to the border, then rejoined U.S. No. 99 which eventually became a freeway. In the north, "I-5" skirted Grants Pass, climbed Mt. Sexton and other ridges, ultimately arriving in the Willamette Valley and on to Portland and Seattle.

The Beekman house was built about 1875 and was acquired by Jackson County in 1959. The house is open to the public in summer, by appointment at other times.

The Rogue River Valley had, since the beginning, been all but cut off from convenient tourist travel because of twisting, old, mountain roads. It was common to require twelve hours to drive from the valley to Portland. Southern Pacific's passenger schedule was nearly a twelve-hour ride as the tracks went up, down, around, about like the road. Medford had one of the first recognized airports in Oregon (1926), but passenger service by air, until the 1960's, wasn't that great either. After 1955, when S.P. stopped its passenger service, the major public transportation was by bus and the torturous snake-like highway. When the freeway opened in the late 1960's, all this changed. Sleepy Jacksonville, and Medford which was quite provincial in its own unique way, suddenly had access to Portland in "jig" time. As an official of the law admonished about the new free(speed)way, "If you get to Portland in less than four hours and five minutes, you're speeding." (At 55 mph it takes a little longer.)

Soon after the freeway opened, the highway people installed signs pointing toward Jacksonville announcing, "NATIONAL HISTORIC LANDMARK." Many, wondering what this was all about left the freeway, drove five miles and, *voila!* They liked what they saw. They found an historic town with original buildings fantastically alive and well.

Many Jacksonville residents seem pretty pleased with their town now

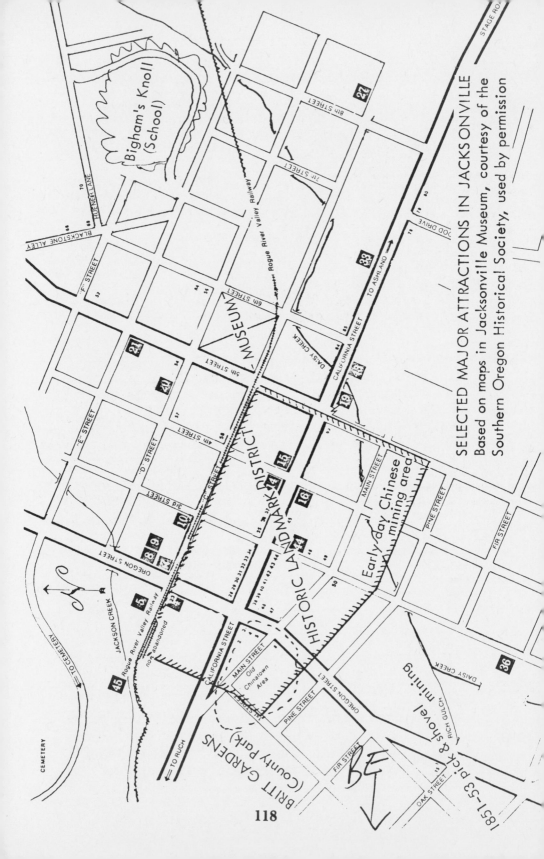

SELECTED MAJOR ATTRACTIONS IN JACKSONVILLE
Based on maps in Jacksonville Museum, courtesy of the
Southern Oregon Historical Society, used by permission

118

Small numbers are historic sites
Large (reversed) numbers are mine locations from 1930's

1. Cemetery 1860
2. Power sub-station 1905
3. Butcher shop1854
4. Orth Bldg 1872
5. Brunner Bldg 1854
8. City Hall 1880
15. Monument: Gold Discovered 1851
23. Rogue River Valley R.R. Depot1891
28. Site of 1st trading tent in town
29. Bella Union Saloon 1856
30. Kennedy's Tin Shop 1861
31. Sach's Bros. Dry Goods 1861
32. Neuber's Jewelry Store (& card room) 1862
33. Sutton's Drug Store c1856
34. Beekman Bldg. Express & Bank 1863
35. United States Hotel 1881
36. H. Judge Harness c1858
37. Ryan & Morgan Gen'l Store 1863
38. Masonic Hall 1875
39. Blacksmith Shop 1859
40. Gunsmith Shop c1858
41. Drum Hotel & Gen. Mdse c1858
42. Anderson & Glenn Gen. Mdse 1856
43. Kubli Bldg 1884
44. Redmen's Hall 1884
45. Wade, Morgan & Co. c1861
46. Table Rock Billiard Saloon 1859
47. McCully Bldg 1855
48. Ryan Hotel Bldg c1856
49. Milo Caton House c1902
52. B. F. Dowell House 1859
54. Methodist Church 1854
57. St. Joseph's Roman Catholic Church 1858
58. Catholic Rectory 1861
64. Armstrong House 1858
65. Presbyterian Church 1881
78. Beekman House 1876
79. Reames House 1868
80. Hattie Reames White House 1891
84. Unidentified House c1880

4. A fellow lived in old Depot, mined behind bldg.
5. Across from Depot two men did nicely.
7. A. C. VanGalder dug pit in backyard, tunneled under "C" St. to Depot. Made excellent money.
8. VanGalder bought house and lot just as two others gave up dud mine—filled hole then planted Redwood tree which still stands.
9. VanGalder dug another shaft. No gold. Dips in lawn at 250 N.Oregon St.are locations of D & E.
14. Two men dug here, tunneled under California Street then under sidewalk. Did well according to former City Mining Inspector.
15. Corner service station and lot was once major mine shaft as well as equipment storage yard for VanGalder and Jack Green who mined at least $25,000 here.
19. Working the creek where service station now stands at 5th and California Sts, two men mined a lot of gold.
20. Behind Methodist Church, water problems caused tunnel to collapse from which miner escaped. A high producing mine until abandoned.
21. "Blackie" Wilson was miner who hired others to assist digging under his garage where pay dirt was excellent.
27. Joe McIntyre agreed to allow a partnership of Frank Taylor, Leonard Osborn and George Campbell to dig for gold on his property if they would not dig within 12-feet of his house. (See copy of contract.)
33. A tunnel went under house where lady complained of hearing noises in the night. The grunts were men taking out excellent pay dirt.
36. Lee Hardy dug several shafts, reported excellent results.
43. Four men operated the "White Owl" mine but did not report their results.
45. Bill Dobbyn and Fred Christean ran a dragline dredge in Jackson Creek from the bridge upstream to where bedrock came to surface. (See text)

that it has official recognition and protection under the preservation measures. But there are others who don't agree with all that's happened to preserve the town's center, possibly because of tax breaks which are a part of it. Jacksonville, say quite a few, is a town in which people try to live normal lives but wonder how to cope with tourists who park on lawns, block driveways, raise dust as they roar through an unpaved public parking lot, plus the impact of huge crowds when special events are staged.

Nevertheless, many have restored older homes just because they think

E.O. "Curley" Graham, Marshal for the Pioneer Day parade, 1982 and Mrs. Graham (top). California Street becomes pedestrian concourse. This 1917 Ford was in parade.

No longer on scheduled runs, the Pioneer Village stage coach might be seen if one is at the right place at the right time.

it's a good idea to protect what they own. The Booster Club provided plaques for older buildings on which the date of construction is stated. At the museum, and at selected places elsewhere, one can obtain a small map for a self-guided walking tour. If the scene is properly set there will be tourists and tourists bring money.

With the town full of people particularly in summer, the 25 mph speed limit is rigidly enforced. There are no parking meters, no stop-and-go signals, and no drive-in fast food joints. It's a town to be enjoyed by walking and looking.

The Jacksonville Museum is an amazing place. At this writing there is no admission charge, and a volunteer welcomes visitors with the request to write names and "where are you froms" in the guest book. It's the way the county keeps tabs on popularity of the museum. Permanent displays include Peter Britt Photography Studio; the judge's desk used in the DeAutremont murder trial; a firearms exhibit is a major drawing card; other displays some permanent and some which change or are "visiting" from outside sources. The museum also has a reference library where professional and amateur historians delve into the nitty-gritty of the past, and without which this book could not have been written.

In an adjoining building—the old county jail—is "Pinto's Theatre." Kids collect here for special events, puppet shows, and where the walls are covered with pictures of "Pinto" and "Bozo-the-Clown" record albums. The kid's section is an exciting learning environment where kids "touch gently and explore a lot." (Don't rush them, dad!)

In summer there are three major events which fill the town to capacity. "Pioneer Days" celebration in June is sponsored, at this writing, by the Volunteer Fire Department. In July it's the Children's Festival sponsored by the Jackson County Library and the Story Telling Guild. In August, the Britt Music Festival commands national attention.

Visitors like "atmosphere" and Jacksonville has it. People like to eat and "J'ville" has restaurants of many varieties—especially the Jacksonville Inn—including small coffee shops. There are antique and gift shops; art galleries; a drug store; the bakery turns out astounding delights; one supermarket (outside the Historic boundary); usual banks, a summer theatre "Melodrama" the Post Office is new: old fashioned fabric and sewing shop; one can look and buy stained glass in leaded frames; leathercraft; and there are "saloons."

Jacksonville, the little town which lost its railroad, lost its county seat, lost its junior and senior high schools and never had an economic base, now makes its history its industry. □

CHAPTER 17

MUSIC UNDER THE STARS

THE BRITT MUSIC FESTIVAL COMMEMORATES PETER BRITT, AND was founded in 1963 by Portlanders John Trudeau, a classical musician and conductor, and Sam McKinney, as advertising man and promoter.

The Festival presents a varied program each summer on a wooded hillside a few blocks from the center of town, which lovers of music enjoy while relaxing on blankets spread on the grass. A few bring lawn chairs and their are some benches. (But no dogs, please.)

Back in 1962 Trudeau and McKinney talked with the Jacksonville City Council, when Curley Graham was mayor, in an effort to convince the council that Jacksonville's spirits would indeed be lifted by such an annual event.

Don Wendt, who was on the council at that time recalls, "...you can imagine the reaction of some of us uncultured council members who were much more familiar with the tunes of the J'ville Tavern's music box than the refined compositions of Bach, Beethoven and others, which Mr. Trudeau wanted to play."

But the council listened as the visitors expounded on the atmosphere, the people and the setting of Jacksonville—especially the hillside known at the Peter Britt property. It sounded good. Wendt continued, "I remember making the motion to accept the offer and the council approved. But little

Britt Festival Symphony directed by John Trudeau, is heard each August by thousands who sit or lounge on a hillside (top). Many at daytime concert bring sack lunches (bottom).

124

John Trudeau, founder of the Britt Music Festival and director of the annual summer symphony.

did I realize the tremendous work" ahead of a lot of people to get it all together. The city didn't own the property. The council set about to show the citizens the need to get behind the effort to have a summer concert. People from all over the valley responded. Wendt wrote in his *Jacksonville Nugget*:

Mrs. Bert Pree was the first president of the Britt Board along with Mr. Graham, Ben Trowbridge, Lee Konschott, Darrell Huson, Lew Tycer, George Brewer, Virginia Lusk, William Mansfield and Myself. We met to decide just where to begin. First the land had to be acquired. Second a pavilion had to be built. Two major undertakings especially when no-one really knew where to start. But there was a cohesion with this group, and things began to percolate when the wheels started. First, materials were donated by merchants all over the valley. Volunteer labor was donated at a fast pace. Before we knew it, the work had begun. I'm sure many don't realize that the first Britt pavilion was built with labor from the Jackson County Prisoners. These men were 'loaned' to us to come each day and work, thanks to the efforts of county Commissioners Ed Taylor and Don Faber. I can remember taking them back to the county jail in the evening.

Progress was really noticeable. I can remember getting a D-4 cat from West Main Rental to help level the ground and make pathways around the pavilion. Even some of the prisoners were talented enough to run the heavy equipment for us. I also remember staying up till the wee hours of the morning with a crew from Pacific Light & Power Company with their auger drilling holes where benches would finally rest in front of the stage. There were many volunteers who with rakes in hand, would line up on top of the hill, and proceed to rake downward all the weeds and leaves around, leaving the grounds clean to allow people to place their blankets and chairs. I remember my father, George Wendt, donating his time for days wiring the new structure so each light would be in its proper place. Even getting water to wetten down the dust was a monumental task.

Examples of postmarks from Jacksonville

Top to bottom (1) Machine cancel with slogan **NATIONAL HISTORIC LANDMARK GOLD DISCOVERED 1851.**

(2) Hand cancel with "OREG." Apr. 27, 1904 on 2ᶜ Scott No. 319 issue of 1903.

(3) Hand cancel with rosette Oct. 17, 1888 on 2ᶜ Scott No. 210 issue of 1883.

(5) Hand cancel Dec. 2 (no year) on 3ᶜ stamped envelope Scott No. U58, a Civil War issue of 1864.

(4) Hand cancel Jan. 6, 1886 on 1ᶜ stamped envelope Scott No. U116 issued in 1874.

But function it did, and when the musicians arrived a few days early, they all had places to stay, mostly in Jacksonville where many local residents opened up their homes to these talented performers. The first night's performance was history. It was superb, not that I or some others really understood the kind of music, but because something great in Jacksonville was happening. The beer and wine flowed after the first performances, as we all knew then that the Peter Britt Music Festival should ever continue.

Twenty years later, the Britt Festival is believed to be the oldest classical festival in the United States. But there are changes in the wind. The community appears split on their likes or dislikes about the Festival. There are well-wishers, but these are now mostly out-of-town people.

Some feel the handling of "The Britt," as it's called, has become high-handed with little concern for the people of Jacksonville. While years of struggle to make the Festival successful have achieved in many areas, others, like public relations with the folks in Jacksonville have not earned high marks. Most local people cannot see Jacksonville becoming another "cultural" center, referring to Ashland's Shakespeare influence.

Initially, nearly all the music was symphonic. In recent years, responding to popular appeal and to gain more hard cash in gate receipts, while remaining predominantly symphonic, other types of music are being added. Of course there are symphonic choirs joining the orchestra but in addition there are piano recitals; vocal soloists; quartets—instrumental and vocal; a Civil War Brass Band using Civil War-era instruments; a solo guitarist; and specialty groups. Some of the small ensembles and soloists are heard in the ballroom of the U.S. Hotel or in the historic sanctuary of the First Presbyterian Church.

Some purists squirmed when they heard that "bluegrass" and "country" music had come to Britt. And Jazz!

In 1981, the season was extended to add both. The programs are not intermixed, as many say they would prefer but it appears that bluegrass and jazz will be permanent additions to the summer's program.

Although these are heralded as separate festivals, each abutts another: Bluegrass, symphony, then jazz festival.

With these styles of music, the Britt Music Festival will become as enticing a lure to Southern Oregon as the Shakespeare Festival in Ashland, with many visitors planning their trips to take in both. Music lovers are now realizing that "The Britt" is the most beautiful as well as diverse music festival in the west. □

"Fred," the friendly dragon eats only one kind of "food"—litter picked up by kids at Children's Festival who take great pride feeding him (top). "Nail-it" project (center) and leathercraft for beginners (bottom) are examples of great experiences planned just for kids.

CHAPTER 18

KIDS IN PETER'S FRONT YARD

WHEN ONE CAN GET A LIBRARY SYSTEM, A PARKS department, the County commissioners and eight local organizations to agree to cooperate, it is truly a "Magical, Wonderful Happening"! The Children's Festival, held at Britt Gardens, a County Park in Jacksonville, is sponsored by the Jackson County Library System and the Medford Storytelling Guild. It is truly an amazing "doing" when thousands of kids get together to "see and do." The Festival has been growing to such an extent that further growth is discouraged.

It all started with the Library System's storytelling program. During the year, moms bring their children, some toddlers, to a special corner in the library junior department once a week to listen to, and watch a story being acted out. Storytellers are usually mothers who have experience reading aloud to their own children. In time, a Storytelling Guild was formed by interested mothers, and others, who enjoy children and use the Guild as a creative outlet. The Children's Librarian coordinates activities. The Guilds are usually small groups where each member is active for the good of the kids. The Guild is not a social organization.

The library furnishes quality paperback picture books rather than have mothers donate supermarket type books.

In areas away from the library, a "Storymobile" makes a regular route throughout the community offering books and stories to children who would not normally reach the library. Children who have never been in the library are the target group. Books are loaned to children during the story hour whether it is in the library or on a front lawn with the Storymobile parked at the curb. In rainy weather, the group of kids and the storyteller might get under a carport.

The summer Children's Festival could be called a climax, for the festival is a "show, feel, try-it-out" experience for the youngsters. It takes a lot of volunteers a long time to hang it all together.

The Children's Festival includes performing arts and manual arts. There is a puppet show from the Pied Piper (portable) Theater Stage. Performers stroll the park performing in impromptu settings as opportunities present themselves. There is a "Storytelling Tree" under which Shakespearean actors volunteer their time to tell stories. Strolling musicians play a well practiced repertoire of folk music. Jugglers give instant lessons. The kids love it all. Clowns meet visitors to the park while children get in line to enter.

Children participate in all activities of the festival including an animal farm where they see and touch live animals and ask questions about them. Animals include horses, cows (with demonstration of how to milk a cow), goats, rabbits, sheep, pigs, ducks, chickens, etc. Some of these might be seen in a zoo, but there is no zoo near Jacksonville so the owners bring them to the Festival. Regular animal food is on hand which the kids feed the animals.

Volunteer mothers, members of the Storytelling Guild, are everywhere for there is much to do.

Other volunteers include gymnasts, magicians, folk singers, dancers, etc. There are square dance clubs, Community Theatre players, and opera singers. Radio and TV personalities are masters of ceremonies.

In the Arts and Crafts section, artists paint while kids watch—then the kids try it themselves.

Professionals who demonstrate their arts are never paid to do so and they do not sell their output at the fair. The whole idea is to offer new and exciting ideas for children who are encouraged to make something by themselves (or with the help of the professionals), which the child takes home at the end of the day.

Arts and crafts for Mother Goose Land (younger children) include hammer and nail building; macaroni bead stringing; paper plate collage; banner painting; work with clay; etc.

For older kids the crafts include: pottery making with clay; macrame; batik; wood carving; candlemaking; jewelry making; leathercraft; sandcasting; paper sculpture; stitchery; and others. There are food-taste experiences in a working exhibit of "Foods from Other Lands."

The library has always played a key role in the success of the Children's Festival. It is the base of operations for planning and organization of the Festival and the Children's Librarian is the library coordinator for the event. The library acts as the sponsoring agency for the Storytelling Guild and is the support body as well as the advisory body for the function.

The first year of the Festival was planned for a small gathering of fifty children, to be held under a tree at Britt Garden. It was billed as "The Best of Storyhour." Six hundred showed up! Fifteen years later, with many of the bugs worked out, there were over 15,000—3,000 at a time in the park in three days. The park is only eleven acres. With this many participants, volunteers are hard put to give equal time to each child. The Festival does *not* promote attendance from outside the county. It is *not* a place for visitors to Jacksonville to "dump" kids for a glorified baby sitting period.

A small gate fee (50ᶜ in 1981) covers operating costs. The adult participants' only reward is the satisfaction of sharing something of themselves with children.

Gathering of the volunteers is a major project but comes easily when people want to provide new ideas for children. The process begins immediately after a July Festival. One area of concern is to identify problems then correct them. Another is to retire played-out volunteers with new people who will fill important shoes. Supplies and equipment must be arranged—either purchased, borrowed or begged. The Children's Festival consumes 2,700 volunteers to accomplish the goal. Local businesses donate materials and services. Many service organizations adopt the Festival as "community service projects." While the major list of volunteers are women, many "handy-helpful-husbands" are included. Boy Scouts are included, for troops as well as individual Scouts work on Community Service projects. The County Parks and Recreation Department keep the major trappings in the County warehouse during the year, and County crews haul the equipment to and from the Britt grounds at Festival time.

The local chapter of the American Association of University Women (A.A.U.W.) has been involved with the event from the start—back when the group planned for only fifty kids—advanced fifty dollars to begin the whole thing.

One of the absolutes of the Festival is the prohibition of fast-food stands. Says a volunteer, "The children are here to see and do, not to stuff themselves on junk foods." The A.A.U.W. has a facility operating independently of the Festival but for the convenience of the Festival, which serves cold drinks (it's usually pretty hot in July) to the kids for a nickel or a dime (and hot sandwiches for hungry daddies and workers). Profits from this one-and-only food concession provide funds to refinish the stand for the next year and to fund scholarships. The partnership of Children's Festival Board and A.A.U.W. works beautifully. A.A.U.W. members also assist in other areas of the Festival as volunteers.

The Children's Festival and Peter Britt Music Festival have been compatible on the same grounds for years—but not at the same time—since the mid-1960's. The concerts started in 1963 and the Children's Festival in 1966. It has taken years to get everything coordinated, but those challenges when reviewed today just bring knowing grins. Examples: Poison oak control; only a single electrical outlet; just one water faucet; had to rent portable "restrooms;" but not really a challenge for just a handful of kids.

Peter Britt loved his children, and he would no doubt smile then shake his head in disbelief if he saw 15,000 in his front yard in just three days in July! □

JACKSONVILLE, OREGON

Appendix A

The discovery of gold in the Rogue River valley attracted, with some well-disposed persons, many of the most unprincipled and ungovernable white men from all countries; with few exceptions, but for these wretches, *it is believed the Indians of Oregon would have been the most peaceable, friendly, and easiest managed, with proper care, of any uncivilized tribes within the bounds of the United States.* It is very true the Rogue river tribe was one of the few exceptions referred to; but they had felt the force of a blow administered by a command under Brevet Major P. Kearny, captain 1st dragoons in 1851, near the mouth of a branch of Rogue River about 15 miles north of Table Rock, and whether this was sufficiently salutary or not, their roguish and stealing propensities afforded no just provocation, more especially when not in the commission of crime, for the infernal acts of cruelty committed upon them by some of that class of unprincipled whites, such as are always known to lurk on the confines of civilization, between the peaceable settlements and the Indian lodge, acknowledging no law but that of force, and in their hearts and acts far deeper down in the scale of human degradation, and far more capable of producing mischief in the settlements, because to an evil heart, there is coupled superior intelligence, than any Rogue River Indian was known to be, before or since the discovery of gold in his valley.

Does any one ask what these infernal acts of cruelty have been? and by whom have they been perpetrated? Official public documents tell us: In the autumn of 1852, "a party of citizens, under conduct of one Captain Ben. Wright, massacred over thirty Indians out of forty-eight, who had come into his camp by invitation to make a "peace."

It seems "Wright determined not to return to Yreka without bearing some evidence of success in his expedition, and having failed to find them by hunting for the Indians, he invited them to his camp by means of a squaw. Upon this invitation forty-eight came, and while there Wright directed his men to charge their rifles afresh, to make a sure fire, which was done in presence of the Indians, without exciting their suspicion, and then, upon a signal from Wright, they suddenly fired upon the Indians, and succeeded in killing about 38. The signal was the discharge of a revolver by Wright, by which he killed the two principal Indians, with whom he had been engaged in talk. Wright's men returned to town, bearing on their rifles the scalps of their victims, he reporting that he had demanded of the Indians stolen property, and on their refusal to deliver it up he had thus punished them."—(Ex. Doc. 76, 34th Cong., 3d session.)

As a natural result of this treachery, the tribe combined with the Rogue River Indians, in the following summer, and attacked a settlement near Jacksonville.

We thus have what are believed to be the provocation and beginning of the Rogue river war of 1853, terminating in a fight between the Oregon volunteers, with one captain and ten soldiers of the United States army, under General Jo. Lane, and the Indians, on the 24th September, 1853, on the side of the mountain to the south of Battle creek.

—T.J. Cram, *Topographical Memoirs*

Appendix B

A HANGING

Among the many trials held in this courtroom, none attracted more attention in their day than that of Louis O'Neil, of Ashland. On November 20, 1884, a grocer of that city, Lewis McDaniel, was killed. He was walking home shortly after dusk. His assailant lay in wait behind a fence and shot him in the head at short range with a shotgun. The subsequent arrest and trial of the alleged murderer was covered to the last detail by both the Jacksonville *Democratic Times* and the Ashland *Tidings*. It appeared to be the last instance of a hanging carried out by a country sheriff, in this case, Sheriff Abraham S. Jacobs.

On November 28, 1884, Louis O'Neill was arrested for the crime. His known enmity to the victim, and his intimacy with the victim's wife made him the logical suspect, but there were no witnesses and the long-drawn out legal proceedings never turned up any but circumstantial evidence. He never confessed to the crime. However, there seemed little doubt that he was guilty. Newspaper accounts state that he did not appear to be surprised when arrested, and did not even inquire as to the charge until later. He was implicated by boot tracks and the murder gun found nearby, which was proven to have been his. The newspapers stated that Mrs. McDaniel showed little grief [over the death of her husband].

O'Neil was tried in Jacksonville Circuit Court before Judge Lionel G. Webster February 27, 1885. He was defended by two of the ablest lawyers in the valley. It took the jury only one hour to render a verdict of guilty. Many ladies attended the trial. On March 22, Judge Webster pronounced sentence, death by hanging in the jail yard while the prisoner still protested his innocence. Motion for a new trial was over-ruled, but O'Neil's lawyers took their case to the Supreme Court. The newspapers commented that the trial was costing a great deal of money, but it would be money "well spent if it dissipates the idea that justice is unable to overtake murderers in Southern Oregon, a natural result of the remarkable disparity between the numbers of murders and the number of convictions."

The Supreme Court upheld Judge Webster's original ruling, and O'Neil was sentenced a second time January 29, 1886. It was now reported that he was getting weak from nervousness and lack of appetite, and "might yet save the sheriff from an unpleasant duty." Meanwhile, the unhappy man was yet hoping they "would find the right man." While trying to prove his innocence he implicated Mrs. McDaniel. She was also arrested and tried for complicity, but was found not guilty. At his second appearance, O'Neil was described as looking in better health than people had been led to expect in view of his threats to starve himself to death. Execution date was set for March 12, and the sheriff requested the Jacksonville Fire Company of 27 men to act as guard. Gallows were erected west of the jail and north of the courthouse, surrounded by a tight board fence 16 feet high. Fifty or sixty people, it was promised, would be admitted. The sheriff announced his intention of performing the task personally. It was agreed that "O'Neil would do some talking now."

A relative of the condemned man, a Mr. Moon, made a desperate last minute trip to Salem to see the governor, but this hope also failed, and on the evening of the last day O'Neil apparently gave up hope. Two Sisters of Mercy from the convent in Jacksonville had been visiting him regularly, and he now asked them to have Father Blanchet call. This the priest did at once, and according to the papers, "it is understood that he made a full confession of his sins."

Tickets were issued to qualified spectators, and the fire company, armed with rifles, presented itself. The spectable was witnessed by about 200, including several women and two or three small children. Before the noose was attached, O'Neil was asked if he had anything to say, the priest spoke out firmly, "Mr. O'Neil has nothing to say." This was construed by the crowd as a virtual confession of guilt.

—Courtesy of Jacksonville Volunteer Fire Dept. (Archives)

ILLUSTRATION CREDITS

Some of the pictures appearing in this book, although credited to others, were made in the author's photolab in Central Point, Oregon from micro-copyfilm to preserve the originals. Photographs not credited were made by the authors.

"Strained determination" is description of effort to have a studio portrait made in the 1880's, simulated here a century later by co-authors Bert and Margie Webber especially for this book.

ABOUT THE AUTHORS

Bert Webber is a research photojournalist whose specialty is what he calls "the fantastic pacific Northwest." He was graduated in Journalism from Whitworth College and he earned his Master of Library Science degree from the University of Portland. He was a school librarian. Bert has written several books all of which have gone into multiple printings. He is also a contributor to newspapers and is listed in *Who's Who in the West* and in *Contemporary Authors*.

Margie Webber is a Registered Professional Nurse who earned her baccalaureate degree in Nursing from the University of Washington. She has worked in a variety of professional nursing positions. In addition, she is a fourth-generation photolab assistant, as well as a copy editor. She has contributed to nursing papers and is co-author, with her husband, of the present volume and of *Beachcombing and Camping Along the Northwest Coast*.

The Webbers, who enjoy working with people, love to travel and do so regularly. They make their home in Oregon's Rogue River Valley—more specifically in the Bear Creek Valley—about five miles from Jacksonville. They have four children and several grandchildren.

For the accompanying photograph, they sought costumes representative of the late nineteenth century, then practiced terse expressions as were frequently the product of turn-of-the-century photographic galleries.

GENERAL REFERENCES

Bancroft, Hubert H. *History of Oregon* Vol XXX (Vol II 1848-1888) 1888

Beeson, Welborn. *Diary of Welborn Beeson, July 22, 1851 - Dec. 31, 1859*

Carey, Charles H. *General History of Oregon* 3rd Ed. Binford, 1971
_____. *A History of the Oregon Constitution* Binford, 1926

Corning, Howard M. *Dictionary of Oregon History* Binford, 1956

Cram, Thos. J. *Topographical Memoir* Ye Galleon 1977

Farnham, Wallace D. *Religion as an Influence in Life and Thought - Jackson County 1860-1890* Unpublished Thesis. U. of Oreg. 1955

Gilmore, Jesse Lee. *A History of the Rogue River Valley, Pioneer Period 1850-1862* Unpublished Dissertation of U. of Calif., 1952

Haines, Francis D. Jr., *Jacksonville, Biography of a Gold Camp* Private Print, 1967
History of Jacksonville Presbyterian Church, Private Print, 1981.

McLeod, Rev. Wm. *History of St. Joseph's Parish, Jacksonville, Oregon 1858-1958* Private Print, 1958

Nelson, Herbert B. *The Literary Impulse of Pioneer Oregon* Oregon State Col., 1948

O'Hara, Edwin V. *Catholic History of Oregon 2nd Ed. Catholic Book Co. 1916*

Oregon; End of the Trail [American Guide Series] Federal Writers' Project. Binford. 1940 Rev. Ed. 1951

Richter, Adam. *A Century of Banking in the Rogue River Valley* Unpublished Thesis, Pacific School of Banking, 1967

Spreen, Christian. *A History of Placer Gold Mining in Oregon 1850-1870* Unpublished Thesis. U. of Oregon, 1939

Sutton, Jack *Indian Wars of the Rogue River* Josephine County Hist. Soc. 1969
_____. *Mythical State of Jefferson* Josephine County Hist. Soc., 1967
_____. *110 Years with Josephine* Josephine County Hist. Soc., 1966

Tucker, William Pierce. *The History of Jackson County, Oregon* Unpublished Thesis Univ. of Wash., 1931

Walling, A.G. *History of Southern Oregon....* Walling 1884

Webber, Bert. *Oregon's Great Train Holdup* (Expanded Ed.) Ye Galleon 1974
_____. *The Hero of Battle Rock* (Expanded Ed.) Ye Galleon, 1978

Listings in *italic* are illustrations

COLOPHON

The JACKSONVILLE, OREGON, THE MAKING OF A NATIONAL HISTORIC LANDMARK *was written on a Remington SR-101 Correctable, Dual-pitch Typewriter by the authors. The photographs in the book are largely the work of Bert Webber using an Olympus OM-1, 35mm camera with assorted lenses and attachments, then he did the picture processing in his Central Point, Oregon, photo-lab.*

The book was printed in the workshop of Glen Cameron Adams, who has been publishing books under the name of Ye Galleon Press for many years, in the sleepy country village of Fairfield, in southern Spokane County in Washington State. Typesetting was done by Miss Kristy Mayfield and Dale La Tendresse using a 7300 Editwriter computer photosetter. The text of the book was set in 12 point Baskerville and the picture legends in 10 point Baskerville Bold. The book title on cover and on title page was set in 48 point Old English by Don Wendt at Wendtco Webb Printing Company in Medford, Oregon, on a Compugraphic 48 computer photosetter. Camera-darkroom work was by Evelyn Foote Clausen. The film was opaqued, plates made and pages printed by Robert La Tendresse, using a 770CD Hamada offset press. The printed sheets were folded by using a multisheet Pitney Bowes folder. Signatures were assembled by Ye Galleon Press staff. General book design was by Bert Webber, supervised by Glen Adams. Co-authors Bert and Margie Webber distributed the pictures throughout the book to match the text, did the final layout, and prepared the index in Central Point, Oregon. Paper stock is 70 pound Lowell Offset Ivory and the ink is Vandijk Brown and Bordeaux Red. Binding was done by Willem Bosch of Oakesdale, Washington. This was a fun project. We had no special difficulty with the work.